Miniature Plants
Indoors & Out

Miniature Plants Indoors & Out

JACK KRAMER

Drawings by Charles Hoeppner

CHARLES SCRIBNER'S SONS
New York

BOOKS BY JACK KRAMER IN THIS SERIES

Water Gardening
Miniature Plants Indoors and Out
Garden Planning for the Small Property
Hanging Gardens
(other titles in preparation)

Contents ✍

Introduction: Small Plants with Big Rewards ✍

There is fascination in all things miniature that is shared by many people. To the gardener, the world of small plants is nature at her best for it is always full of surprises and beauty. For the apartment dweller, lilliputian plants are very desirable to provide a handsome greenery in a small place. Here he can enjoy flowers and foliage he would otherwise be unable to see. Roses, orchids, geraniums, cacti, succulents, and a host of other plants offer tiny replicas of their bigger cousins.

Small herb gardens are for the gourmet-minded, bottle gardens and terrariums are for the curious, and vivariums with tiny plants and animals keep children occupied for hours. For hobbyists with limited space, growing miniatures under artificial light has special rewards.

For the homeowner with a small plot of ground—and who can afford large properties these days?—gardens of small plants are practical, sometimes the only way to have plants. There are lovely tiny phlox, impatiens, and other miniature and dwarf annuals and perennials with new ones introduced frequently. Dwarf trees and shrubs are also part of the outdoor picture to be used with flowers, or by themselves, for a low maintenance garden. Wall gardens with diminutive plants present other possibilities. Not to be forgotten are sink gardens and lovely miniature bulbs, the harbingers of spring that can be used in many situations.

Small plants—miniature or dwarf—offer an avenue of gardening for young or old, for apartment dweller or suburban gardener. And many times the small plants outshine their larger counterparts. With little plants troubles are small too, so, if your gardening time is precious, these are plants for you.

The plants in this book may be small, but they offer a close look at nature with big rewards of beautiful flowers and handsome greenery. Indoors or out you will find many places for miniature plants to brighten the scene and add pleasure to daily living.

—Jack Kramer

Miniature Plants
Indoors & Out

1. Presenting the Miniatures ✍

Roses and orchids are generally thought of as standard-sized plants, but these groups and other plant families—begonias, geraniums, and so on—all have diminutive members just as beautiful as their larger counterparts.

Some plants are true miniatures, and others are dwarfs. Sizes vary with the kind of plant: a miniature orchid may be two inches high, while a dwarf shrub may be three feet or more. I have not tried to establish restrictive dimensions; sizes for miniatures, dwarfs, and small plants are always debatable. I have often included a twelve-inch plant because it was just too good not to mention.

Miniature plants have infinite charm and there are all kinds for every type of indoor gardener: button fern in a glass garden, tiny palms in a dish garden, or bright, tiny flowers of small geraniums or begonias at the window.

You also can grow miniatures under artificial light in a space no larger than a closet, and, of course, miniature flower arrangements that accent a coffee table or desk are always a unique decoration.

Miniatures are versatile plants that have advantages over standard-sized plants. They are lightweight, need only small quantities of soil, are small enough so that attacks by insects are never a big problem, and, if lost from neglect, are expendable.

Each plant family has its own charm, idiosyncrasies, and requirements. At first, you may want to grow a few from several plant

A window garden of small plants can be a lovely addition to a room. Here semperflorens *begonias and ivy thrive in handsome white pots.* Photo by Roche.

Even a tea cup makes a home for lilliputian plants; Saxifraga sarmentosa "Tricolor" is the accent plant. Photo by Joyce R. Wilson.

families. Later, you may find a favorite and collect only them. Miniature geraniums have captured the interest of a friend of mine. He has an extensive collection, knows all about them, but is always searching for more.

I have grown more than a hundred tiny orchids because I find their diminutive flowers enchanting. Whatever group of plants you choose, you will find enough varieties to keep you busy for years, and, like small children, small plants are full of surprises. Some cacti have flowers four inches in diameter on a two-inch plant, and many orchids do not have a single bloom as we know it, but dozens of wee flowers that form one large one.

2

WINDOW GARDENS

Standard plants, because of their size, are more suitable as room accents in ornamental containers; at windows too often they appear awkward and unattractive. A window that accommodates a half-dozen large plants can provide space for eighteen miniatures, and you still will be able to see through the glass.

It is easier to achieve good window compositions with a group of *small* plants. You can rearrange them at will without undue effort, and there is a wide variety of colors, textures, and shapes to work with. Never crowd plants in any situation; let each one speak for itself. Fill metal or plastic trays (available at suppliers) with a bed of crushed gravel and set pots on top.

Try to place plants of the same group together to provide a more attractive and interesting scene. If you have four shelves, use one for geraniums, one for orchids, and so forth. Placement of your miniature plants depends on your individual situation; however, they should be near light, close to a water supply, and where they can be seen and appreciated.

Select plant containers with care; don't be satisfied with just anything. Some have character that is more in keeping with a kitchen setting, and more ornate containers are better in the living room. Plastic pots, especially the colored ones, are attractive, as are small Spanish terra-cotta pots. Try for a handsome harmony of color, plant, and container.

Place window plants according to their requirements: some like shade and others will thrive in sunlight. Follow this list for success. (See Chapter 5 for other plants.)

Plants for Sunny Exposures:

Azalea "Gumpo"—delightful, with frilled red flowers
Bambusa nana—fine grassy plant
Bertolonia maculata—dark green, silver, and red foliage
Chlorophytum bitchetti—fine trailer, with green and yellow foliage
Coleus rehneltianus—brightly colored plant
Crossandra infundibuliformis—shiny green leaves and orange blossoms
Exacum affine—gentian with blue flowers

Impatiens "Elfin"—dark green leaves and brick red flowers
Kalanchoë blossfeldiana—many varieties; red flowers
Pellionia daveauana—elliptical dark, bronzy, olive green foliage
Rhipsalidopsis rosea—robust plant with rose pink blooms
Streptocarpus rexii—pale orchid flowers with purple throat

Plants for Shady Exposures:

Aglaonema pictum—blue green leaves splashed with silver
Anthurium scherzerianum—lovely green leaves and red bracts
Caladium humboldtii—deep green leaves marked with silver
Chamaeranthemum igneum—velvety, bronze green leaves with pink
    veining
Columnea microphylla—tiny leaves and bright red flowers
Cryptanthus—many varieties; all highly colored
Fittonia verschaffeltii—iridescent foliage
Hedera helix—large group of fine ivies
Microlepia setosa—lovely fern-type plant
Pellionia repens—metal green foliage
Peperomia caperata—one of the many fine small peperomias
Pilea—many fine varieties; creepers
Saxifraga sarmentosa—small begonia-like leaves; popular

UNDER ARTIFICIAL LIGHT

If you do not have window space, you can grow miniature plants
under artificial light without any sunlight. Standard-sized plants are
often grown under lights too, but miniatures (to my way of thinking)
are better because they stay small and never become unsightly or
crowded.

I have seen many fine gardens under lights; one was in a tiny space
in a Chicago apartment, another was in the attic of a house, and I
had a light garden for my orchids on a bedside table for many years.
If you do not want the expense of a garden cart or tray, a few African

*Many miniatures decorate this delightful window garden; plants are in terra-
cotta pots, many of them in a galvanized tray set an inch above the radiator
top. Photo by Gottscho-Schleisner.*

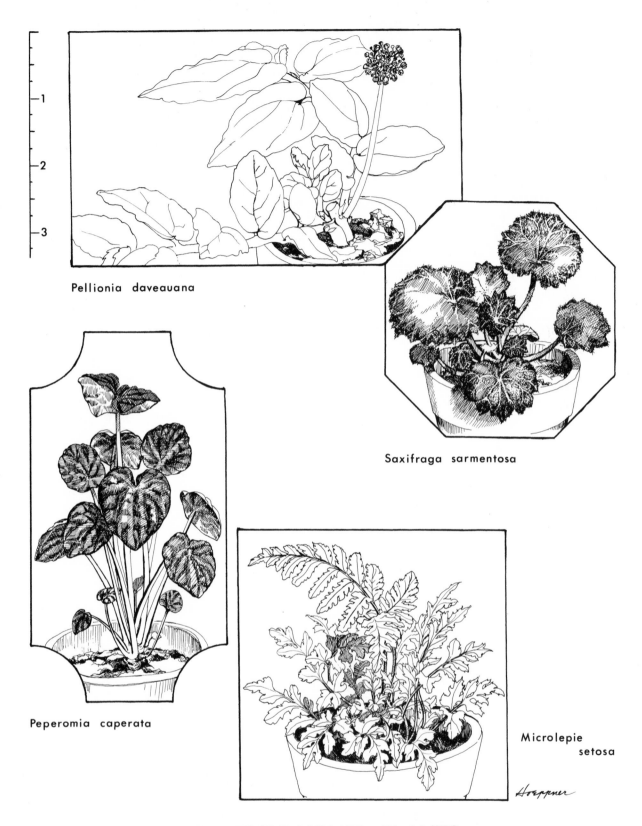

Pellionia daveauana

Saxifraga sarmentosa

Peperomia caperata

Microlepie
setosa

Hoeppner

MINIATURE HOUSE PLANTS

African violets occupy the top tray of an indoor light garden; they are placed on white gravel in plastic trays. The light garden unit is available from suppliers. Photo courtesy of Sylvania Electric.

violets under existing fluorescent lamps on a kitchen counter can be desirable.

Fluorescent and incandescent (reading) lights are generally used by indoor gardeners because they are cheap, available, and, until more is known about plants and light, the most beneficial. You can use standard fluorescent lamps or the lamps especially designed for plant growth: Gro Lux by Sylvania Electric Company and Plant Gro by Westinghouse Electric Company. Incandescent light is another source for plant light; a combination of both types of light is generally considered best for plant growth.

There are table models and carts specifically designed for plants under lights. Basically, these consist of adjustable reflector canopies that direct the light on the plants, trays, and electrical connections for fluorescent lamps and incandescent lamps. Before selecting a unit, be sure that it has an adjustable canopy, rustproof or made of rust-resistant materials, and that it provides sufficient light—fifteen to twenty watts of illumination per square foot of growing area. (This is minimum light intensity for most plants.)

Light is necessary for photosynthesis—the production of sugar and starches from carbon dioxide and water. The visible spectrum, like a rainbow, has colors ranging from red to violet with wave lengths ranging from 3,800 to 7,000 angstroms. (An angstrom denotes the length of light waves.) Research indicates that plants require blue, red, and far-red to produce normal growth; blue enables them to manufacture carbohydrates, red controls the assimilation and effects the response to the relative length of light and darkness, and far-red works in conjunction with red. Plants thrive when they receive sufficient levels of blue and red light and adequate balances of far-red light. This light is supplied by fluorescent and incandescent lamps.

Plants such as orchids, geraniums, cacti, and succulents need a great deal of light—at least four forty-watt fluorescent lamps. Others, such as African violets and begonias, flourish under a two-lamp setup of eighty watts, and tiny foliage plants like ferns, pilea, and peperomia will, if necessary, survive lower-light levels.

The subject of artificial light and plants is varied and vast, and for full coverage of this fascinating gardening I suggest the following books: *Fluorescent Light Gardening* by Elaine Cherry (Van Nostrand Reinhold Co.) or *Gardening Under Lights* by Elvin McDonald (Doubleday).

2. Dish Gardens 🍂

Any group of small living plants in a container is a dish garden. These are diminutive scenes of miniature plants arranged to simulate natural landscapes (or occasionally, as with herbs, merely an easy way to grow them).

The miniature replica of nature can be woodland, tropical, or desert in theme. (Do decide on a dominant theme for the garden rather than having a mixture of unrelated plants because in the dish garden each plant is important to the whole.) Miniature compositions are always under close scrutiny, so the garden must be distinctive and created with care. Plants, containers, and design should be chosen so that they complement each other and are pleasing to the eye. To create a successful dish garden—a pleasing, finished picture of harmony and balance of plants, container, and textures—requires some skill and talent.

There is no set rule about the size or shape of the container. It can be round, square, rectangular, or elliptical in shape, but it must be deep enough for at least four inches of soil. Search for an interesting container; glass lamp shades, tea or coffee cups, soufflé dishes, soup bowls, and fluted baking dishes are good choices, as is a simple metal pan or galvanized tray in a woven bread basket or rattan bowl. Match the plant to the container. For example, in the fluted dish grow bold, round-leaved plants; in the tea cup plant the charming, miniature gloxinia and baby's tears; and for a large white bowl, try cacti and succulents with their round sculptural leaves.

Place dish gardens in any room in any place—on a bedside table, mantel, or coffee table, in a bookcase shelf, or on a windowsill. To

protect surfaces from moisture stain, use decorative tablemats. (I water dish gardens at the sink and let them drain a few minutes; even so, there is always some moisture seepage later.)

Miniature gardens are for accent; they are like pictures on the walls. Do not fret if they do not last a lifetime, for they will outlast a dozen roses or a gift plant and usually cost much less. However, if you happen to be penurious like me and want them to last a long time, keep them near windows so that they'll get light.

PUTTING THE GARDEN TOGETHER

To start the dish garden, tease the plants from their individual containers—don't pull them out—and set them in place. Arrange and rearrange until you are satisfied with their positions. Firm the soil around the collar of the plant to support it. Put in trailers and ground covers last. Water the garden so that the soil is barely moist, but don't place it in sunlight; wait a few days before setting the container in light.

Trim plants so that they have sculptural growth. For instance, the dwarf pomegranate (*Punica granatum* var. *nana*) is a fine dish-garden subject since it can be pruned to a desired shape without harm, or use the bold foliage of the peperomia against the graceful fronds of a fern, with a feathery yellow green *Asparagus sprengeri* (emerald fern) in front of a dark green, bold plant like *Kalanchoë blossfeldiana*. For a striking effect, set the accent plant in a bed of white sand or colored gravel.

A flat design with level grading of earth is dull; use hills and valleys. Shape the contour of the soil so that it is interesting and pleasing. Make the front of the garden low, and mound the soil in the rear. Set a plateau of soil and pieces of flat shale in a corner. There are many variations if you use some imagination.

Select the appropriate soil for the plants. My standard potting mix for most plants is one part garden loam, one part sand, and one part

Top left: *Miniature succulents are always handsome. Here they are used in a dish garden arrangement in a handmade cement tray.* Photo by Joyce R. Wilson.

Bottom left: *Echeverias appear like jade roses in this handsome dish garden.* Photo by Joyce R. Wilson.

Materials needed for the dish garden include soil, charcoal chips (in bag), shards for drainage, and small pebbles to decorate top of garden. Note plants in two-inch pots. Photo by author.

leaf mold. To this mix I add more sand for succulents and cacti, and more loam for moisture-loving plants like ferns and mosses. For miniature bromeliads and orchids I use a pocket of fir bark.

A word about package mixes. They may be suitable for some plants, but often they are too muddy, so be sure the mix is porous and has open texture.

Try to keep the soil always evenly moist; this is not easy for what looks moist on top may be bone dry at the bottom. I poke my finger deep into the soil, trying not to dislodge any plants, to test for moisture. Then I know if I should water the garden.

When you water the garden, do not dump water into the dish or you will dislodge plants and soil. Pour water gently from a spout can.

Spray foliage regularly to keep it dust-free and fresh. Pick off faded flowers and dead leaves. Keep the piece attractive. If plants are getting straggly and unattractive, trim them ruthlessly. I have no qualms about this; most house plants are tough and recover quickly with fresh new growth. Fragile though they may seem, I can assure you that plants want to live.

Generally, living room temperatures—72° to 80°F. during the day, 62° to 72°F. during the night—are fine for most dish gardens.

PLANTS

A multitude of miniature plants and the seedlings of mature ones can be used for dish gardening. Most are at florist shops; others are available from mail-order firms. There are trees, flowering plants, foliage gems, and even water plants. Definitely select plants that grow slowly, and choose species that are compatible. Ferns and

Here drainage material (shards) is put in place in dish garden container; note pedestal stand under container. Photo by author.

Drainage material, charcoal chips, and soil have been put in garden; plants are now being arranged after they have been removed from tiny pots (at right). Photo by author.

mosses need a rich soil and shade; flowering plants require a few hours of daily sunlight and a standard soil; and desert plants, such as some crassulas and cacti, need a sandy soil and quite a lot of sunlight. One of my objections to florists' dish gardens—lovely though they may be—is that too often they do not contain compatible plants. A few species will thrive in the sunlight, but other plants will die; thus, the garden must be redone. And by all means, do not crowd plants; give them room to grow.

As mentioned, select a theme for the garden so that it is easy to create a harmonious, pleasing arrangement.

Plants for Warm Locations (78°F. day, 65°F. night):

Aerangis friesiorum (orchid)   *Cryptanthus roseus pictus*
Anthurium scherzerianum   *Episcia dianthiflora*
Begonia dregei   *Ficus pumila* var. *minima*
B. foliosa   *Fittonia verschaffeltii*

Fragaria indica   Sansevieria "Hahni"
Maranta leuconeura var. *kerchoveana*   *Scilla violacea*
Punica granatum var. *nana*   Syngonium "Green Gold"

Plants for Cool Locations (70°F. day, 58°F. night):

Allophytum mexicanum   *Iris flavissima*
Alternanthera bettzickiana   *Juniperus communis* var. *compressa*
Cissus striata   *Manettia bicolor*
Cyclamen neapolitanum   Narcissus (miniature)
Dianthus   *Oxalis herrerae (henrei)*
Exacum affine   Phlox "Ronsdorf Beauty"
Ficus pumila var. *minima*   *Saxifraga sarmentosa*
Gentiana farreri   *Selaginella kraussiana brownii*
Hedera helix   *Viola nana* var. *compacta*

TROPICAL GARDENS

In tropical dish gardens you can use all kinds of small tropical plants to create a lush effect; although you do not want a crowded scene, you do want many plants. Use creeping ground cover and miniature ferns, orchids, and bromeliads. The terrain should be hilly,

The plants in this finished dish garden are tiny ferns, Acorus, and a small-leaved philodendron. Top of the garden has colored stone and Japanese oval rocks for decoration. Photo by author.

and this garden is better without figurines or props. Use a standard soil except for the orchids and bromeliads. (They will need pockets of osmunda or fir bark, or you can leave them in the tiny pots they come in and sink pot and all in the soil. But crack the pot first and settle it into position.)

Select plants from previous lists. (Also see Chapter 5.)

WOODLAND GARDENS

Woodland gardens are a popular scene, always green and inviting and especially cheerful on gray, winter mornings. Put in a few stepping stones and some interesting small stones. Use a rather large container, such as a baking dish or shallow casserole. Plan hills and valleys with gentle slopes. If you want to be fancy, sow some grass seed; it can be trimmed with manicure scissors. Use interesting house plants, such as *Acorus gramineus* and Selaginella species, that can grow in cool and somewhat shady conditions. Miniature African violets and begonias are other good choices for this garden.

DESERT GARDENS

Desert landscapes of cacti and succulents need sunlight, warmth, and sandy soil. Use a pottery container of any shape, but make sure it is deep enough for four inches of soil. Keep the soil rather dry, never wet. Put a few white marble chips on top of the garden for color and perhaps an interesting small stone at one edge for contrast. In most cases, do not expect flowers. However, the interesting shapes and growth of desert plants make them worthwile. These gardens can remain in the same container for several years without replacing the plants. The best plants for a desert garden follow. (See Chapter 5 for more plants.)

Adromischus maculatus	*Mammillaria voburnenis*
Astrophytum myriostigma	*Monanthes polyphylla*
Crassula platyphylla	*Pachyphytum oviferum*
C. schmidtii	*Rebutia kupperiana*
Echeveria tolucensis	*Sedum dasyphyllum*
Gasteria lilliputana	*S. greggii*
Haworthia tessellata	Sempervivum
Maihuenia poepigii	(many kinds)

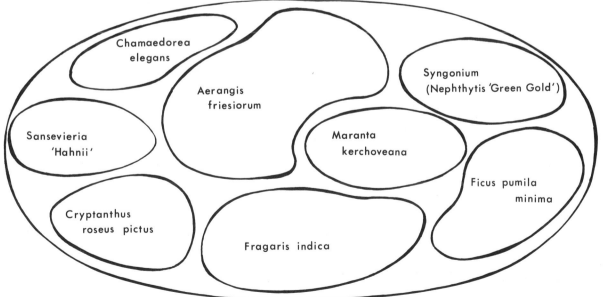

Chamaedorea
elegans

Aerangis
friesiorum

Syngonium
(Nephthytis 'Green Gold')

Sansevieria
'Hahnii'

Maranta
kerchoveana

Ficus pumila
minima

Cryptanthus
roseus pictus

Fragaris indica

HOW TO MAKE A TROPICAL DISH GARDEN

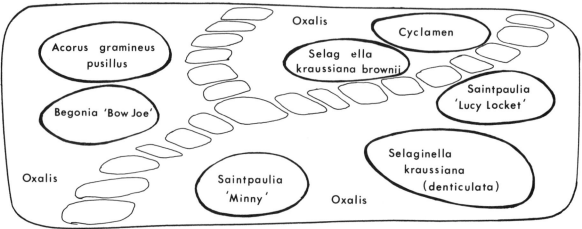

Oxalis

Acorus gramineus pusillus

Selag ella kraussiana brownii

Cyclamen

Begonia 'Bow Joe'

Saintpaulia 'Lucy Locket'

Oxalis

Saintpaulia 'Minny'

Oxalis

Selaginella kraussiana (denticulata)

HOW TO MAKE A WOODLAND DISH GARDEN

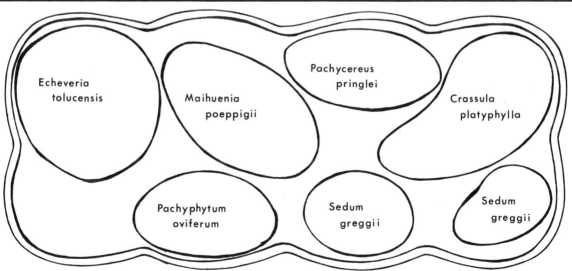

Echeveria
tolucensis

Maihuenia
poeppigii

Pachycereus
pringlei

Crassula
platyphylla

Pachyphytum
oviferum

Sedum
greggii

Sedum
greggii

HOW TO MAKE A DESERT DISH GARDEN

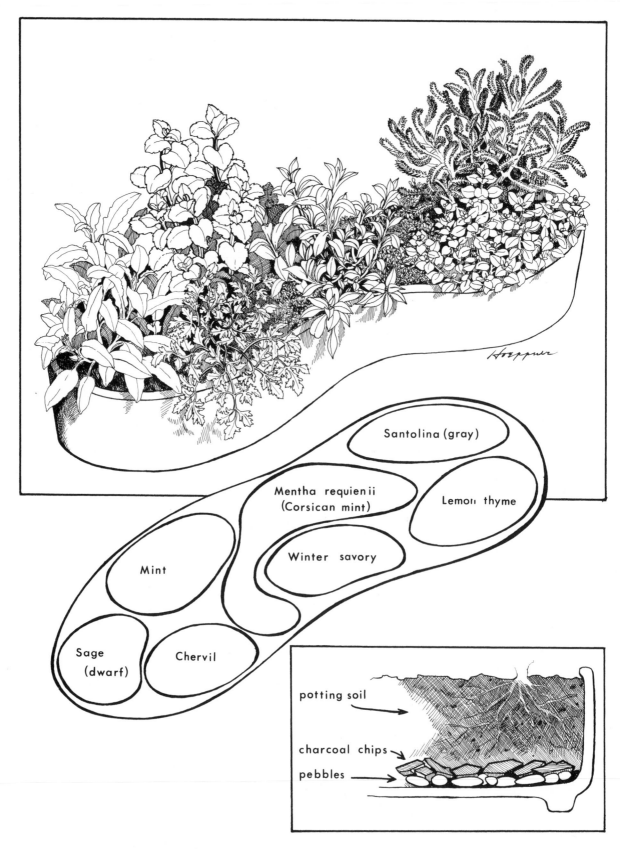

Santolina (gray)

Mentha requienii
(Corsican mint)

Lemon thyme

Winter savory

Mint

Sage
(dwarf)

Chervil

potting soil

charcoal chips
pebbles

HOW TO MAKE A HERB DISH GARDEN

HERB GARDENS

Herbs make a wonderful small garden that can be tucked on a windowsill or even on a back doorstep. Many herbs are ideal small plants that rarely grow over twelve inches and provide beauty as well as fragrance and, of course, seasoning for recipes.

In my garden (see drawing) I have used Santolina for decoration because it is so handsome and winter savory, which grows to ten inches, because it is a fine seasoning for many vegetables. Our plants of lemon thyme and Corsican mint are for fragrance; even if you brush them with your fingers, they give a fine sweet scent. Mint (Mentha) is used for teas and seasoning, and chervil, which grows to twelve inches, is also for seasoning.

This garden does well in a bright window at average room temperatures.

3. *Glass Gardens* ✐

Although they have many indoor uses, miniature plants are perhaps most fascinating in glass gardens where they create diminutive landscapes that are replicas of outdoor scenes. Miniature conservatories are a wonderful way to study nature closely, and they provide hours of fascinating viewing for children and adults as well as a place to grow almost carefree plants. Gardening in glass containers is popular because you only need a few plants, a handful of soil, and your imagination. The garden may be covered with a dome or in a bottle with a stopper, or it can be a scene in a bowl or globe. In either situation it is the placement and the choice of plants that make the little landscape enchanting; there are hundreds of plants to choose from. (The principle of the glass garden is that moisture produced by evaporation condenses on the sides of the container and trickles into the soil, thus saving you the bother of constant watering.)

A container for a glass garden can be anything from a discarded pickle jar to an elegant decanter or brandy snifter; apothecary and candy jars, chemist's flasks, and empty water bottles are other potential glass-garden containers.

How to Make the Garden

An inexpensive goldfish bowl is a good container to start with. To prepare it for planting, spread some shredded sphagnum moss on the bottom and add about one-half inch of gravel for drainage and some charcoal granules to keep the soil sweet. Pour in soil to a depth of several inches, in proportion to the size of the bowl. The type of plant will determine the soil needed. Ferns and mosses prefer an acid mix, cacti and succulents need a sandy soil, and geraniums and gesneriads like a somewhat heavy, rich soil.

Carefully fill the container with soil; if you dirty the inside of the glass, it is difficult to clean, especially the narrow-mouthed containers like flasks and bottles.

Decide what kind of scene you want and place plants accordingly. The woodland garden requires certain plants, the desert scene other species, and so on. Open gardens will need watering, but don't let the soil get soggy. Covered gardens create their own moisture and need only occasional watering.

Bottle gardens (this includes plants in chemist's flasks, purified water bottles, and stoppered containers) are more difficult to assemble than gardens in a bowl, but they are more fascinating. The narrow neck of the container—usually one to two inches in diameter—makes this a challenging project, for people will always ask, "How did you get the plants inside?" You can answer, "With unique tools, a steady hand, and infinite patience."

This glass garden uses miniature Selaginella and ferns as accents. Pebbles and a few large stones are strategically placed to give the garden the appearance of a natural scene. Photo by author.

Small house plants and wild strawberry make this glass garden unique. The container is a pickle jar. Photo by author.

To prepare the bottle garden, cover the base of the container with tiny stones mixed with charcoal granules. Tip the bottle from side to side to get coverage. With a kitchen funnel add dry soil that will flow through the funnel into position without spattering the sides of the container. To make holes in the soil for plants, use wooden chopsticks, knitting needles, or any long and narrow stick. To set plants one-half inch deep in the soil, use a pickup tool (available at local hardware stores) that has a flexible length and a claw at one end which can be controlled by a plunger at your end. If you cannot find the pickup tool, make a device from a long piece of wire. Loop it at the end to hold the plant collar; insert the plant in the soil and

23

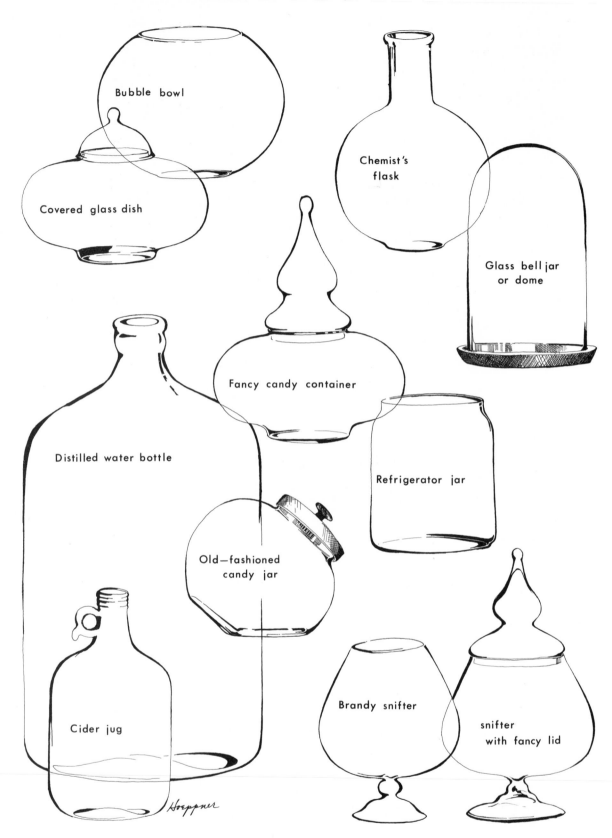

Bubble bowl

Covered glass dish

Chemist's flask

Glass bell jar or dome

Fancy candy container

Distilled water bottle

Refrigerator jar

Old—fashioned candy jar

Cider jug

Brandy snifter

snifter with fancy lid

Hoeppner

GLASS CONTAINERS

remove the tool. Unfortunately, this method is difficult because the wire invariably catches on the plant, so it is hard to remove without pulling up the plant.

Once plants are in place, tamp down the soil with the ends of the chopstick or knitting needle so that the soil is firm around the collar of the plant. Brush excess dirt off plant foliage with an artist's paintbrush. Now the bottle is ready for water, but do not just dump it into the container or the soil and plants will be misplaced. Funnel water slowly into the garden, so that it does not disturb the planting or the soil. Place the garden in a semishaded place, and in about a week or so move it to brighter light. If the soil gets soggy and too much moisture collects on the glass, mildew and rot will occur, so merely uncover the garden—remove the lid or stopper—for an hour or so daily to allow the inside to dry out.

You can also start a bottle garden by sprinkling seeds on the soil. As seedlings grow, pull out the smaller ones and keep only a few plants growing. This is an easy way to get children to start gardens, but it is actually more difficult than assembling a complete garden with plants because it takes much time to remove unwanted seedlings and often it is harder to get seeds to germinate.

Every month or so faded flowers, decayed twigs, and leaves will have to be removed from the bottle garden. This is not easy, so use the pickup tool or an artist's X-Acto knife and proceed carefully,

An old-fashioned candy jar without a lid is home for a thriving coleus; Baby's tears is the ground cover. Photo by author.

Bubble bowls are inexpensive and are fine containers for miniature plants. These gardens require water a few times a week. Photo by author.

trying not to disturb the plantings. Remember that it takes time to keep a bottle garden neat and attractive, but it is well worth the effort.

After a few years plants in the bottle garden will outgrow their quarters, and replanting will be necessary. Do not try to dump the contents out of the bottle; this will not work since the plants are now large. To remove a plant without harming it, draw it up by the roots with the wire or pickup tool, and let the foliage bunch together and pass through the neck of the bottle. Allow the container soil to dry out completely; then turn the bottle upside down, remove the soil, and wash the container.

Left: *Dome gardens make charming room additions and take little space. Plants rarely need water as the garden supplies its own moisture through natural condensation. Photo by author.*

PLANTS FOR GLASS GARDENS

Because there are so many miniatures for glass gardens, do not buy ordinary ones. Seek the unique; search for just the right plant to make the garden extraordinary. Investigate orchids, begonias, and geraniums—all fine plants for gardens; look for tiny ferns (appealing in glass containers), and use seldom-seen mosses such as lycopodiums.

Different plants have different light and soil requirements, so choose plants that will grow well together in the same container. Ferns and mosses like cool and shady conditions; cacti and succulents need a somewhat dry, sunny environment. Flowering plants, such as geraniums and orchids, will need a sunny, moderately moist garden.

You can buy many plants at local nurseries; even the smallest florist shop has a house plant section. Miniature orchids, begonias, and geraniums should be purchased from mail-order suppliers in spring or fall, if possible, because summer heat desiccates plants and in winter there is a possibility of receiving frozen plants.

Ferns are wonderful plants for backgrounds in miniature gardens because their graceful fronds and emerald color are perfect foils for other wee plants. Some true, tiny ferns, such as *Pellaea rotundifolia* (button fern) and *Camptosorus rhizophyllus* (walking fern), are excellent choices, and seedlings of large ferns can be used too. Tuck them in pockets of soil between small stones, or place them on the sides of the tiny hills that you have created in the garden. At ground level the beauty of the diminutive ferns is lost, and you need the graceful flowing lines of the fronds to accent the gardens.

Adiantum hispidulum and *A. bellum* are popular ferns—green and graceful, yet easy to grow. *Humata tyermannii* is another good glass-garden choice, as is *Polystichum tsus-sinense*. (See Chapter 5 for descriptions of miniature ferns.)

We usually think of palms as large plants that need space to grow, but some of the smaller species and seedlings will add grace to the tiny garden and grow for several years before they become too large for the container.

Chamaedorea elegans var. *bella*, the miniature palm, has an overall lacy appearance; *C. cataractarum*, hard to find, is worth the search, for it is a natural dwarf and an amenable plant. *Chamaerops humilis*, the fan palm, is graceful and green, and *Cocos weddelliana* is tree-

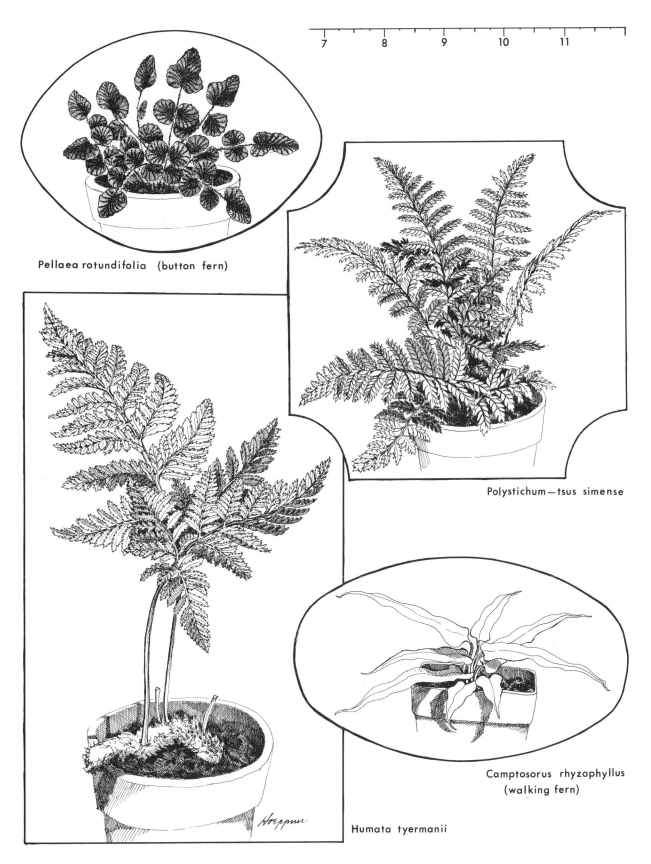

Pellaea rotundifolia (button fern)

Polystichum—tsus simense

Camptosorus rhyzophyllus
(walking fern)

Humata tyermanii

MINIATURE   FERNS

like with slender leaves (look for seedlings of this one). *Phoenix roebelenii* is the popular date palm and, although somewhat large, another good garden choice. Young specimens of *Caryota mitis* and *C. plumosa*, the fishtail palms, can also be used effectively in the glass garden.

Foliage Plants

Foliage plants are the backbone of the glass garden and can be used with abandon. Most appreciate the warm atmosphere of a closed container and will thrive. Some, such as *Aglaonema pictum*, Caladium, *Calathea bachemiana, Chamaeranthemum igneum*, and Cryptanthus species, have variegated foliage; Ficus, Hedera, Pellionia, and Peperomia species have lovely small green leaves. There are many species within each group that are suitable for gardens, and most are available at local florist shops. Foliage plants do not need too much light and, if necessary, can survive untoward conditions. (See Chapter 1 for additional plants.)

Flowering Plants

Flowering plants are for color and brightness. Most must have at least three to four hours of sunlight to bloom. They are more difficult to grow than foliage plants, but the exquisite flowers are worth the extra trouble. Azalea "Gumpo" is a favorite, with its bright red flowers, and *Crossandra infundibuliformis*, bearing orange blossoms, is sure to please. *Exacum affine* gives a blue color to the miniature scene, and *Schizocentron elegans* bears lovely magenta blooms and tiny, handsome, dark green leaves; it is a fast trailer and perfectly suitable for the cool garden. Oxalis species and *Rhipsalidopsis rosea*, adorned with pink blooms when only a few inch tall, are other excellent choices. (See Chapter 1 for additional plants.)

The Vivarium

There is no better way to observe the balance of nature than in a vivarium—a case with living plants and small animals. In this balanced environment flora and fauna complete the life cycle day after day, week after week. Vivariums furnish hours of nature study right in your own home in a small space.

There are many containers for vivariums, but generally an aquarium is the best. Aquariums are readily available, come in many sizes, have sufficient space, and allow an undistorted view of animals and plants. (Space is important, for the animals need room to move about.)

Start with a clean container, place gravel or stone chips on the bottom, and cover with fine sand to a two-inch depth. Scatter some charcoal granules over this, and then add the appropriate soil for the kind of garden you want. Use a sandy mix for the desert scene with lizards and succulent plants. In the woodland garden, where newts and frogs, mosses and ferns thrive, use a rich soil.

Build up soil in the terrarium; create hills and valleys for interest. If you need a small water pond, sink a glass dish into the soil and edge it with tiny stones. Select your plants and place them so that they have space to grow.

After the garden is planted and the soil is moistened, put the animals in the vivarium and cover it with a pane of glass or wire mesh to keep pets in and enemies out (the cover should allow some air to circulate). Except for the desert scene, which needs sunlight and heat, gardens require shady and cool conditions.

There is an array of tiny creatures to fill your gardens and to complete the landscape picture. Chameleons and salamanders will settle happily into a vivarium. Salamanders like to crawl under objects and to hide, so provide small stones and natural crannies for them. Chameleons, on the other hand, like to climb, so put some small branches and twigs in their garden.

Geckos are attractive lizardlike animals with patterned skins of pinkish beige and black. They have large heads and long tongues, and they are beneficial, eating a host of insects, well worth their keep in the vivarium. Geckos prefer a dry environment, so they are well suited to the desert scene. They love to sun themselves on stones and will need a clean dry sand section in one area of the case.

Newts are small animals with tiny crocodile-like feet; they are colorful and at home in a moist and watery woodland or big garden. They are curious and usually quite active.

Toads and frogs can also be placed in a woodland or bog garden that is moist and shady. They need a somewhat large case, for they exercise a great deal; if they disappear for a few days, do not fret, because it is normal for them to hibernate at certain times of the year.

A vivarium includes rocks, stone, plants, and wee creatures. Here a salamander takes his nap on a rock. Photo by Joyce R. Wilson.

All these small creatures and food for them can be purchased at pet stores. Remember that you must supply food and drink for them; this is your responsibility, but luckily is just about all you have to do for them. Never put an animal in a tightly confined space; they need room to move around.

4. Bonsai-type Growing ✐

True oriental bonsai is an art. These miniature plants (sometimes centuries old) in handsome containers are as beautiful as a painting and as dramatic as a piece of sculpture. Bonsai is a three-dimensional form of art that relies on perfect composition and principles of design. Every facet of the composition—leaf, twig, flower—is vital to the overall effect. There is much to be learned in these miniature trees—design, composition, horticulture, and a reverence for patience.

Original bonsai trees and containers are virtually impossible to buy. However, this does not mean you should abandon bonsai growing, for just as we have taken Japanese flower arrangement and molded it to our own tastes, we can also adapt bonsai to our own materials and plants to create charming and rewarding gardens. Indeed, many of our native plants are immensely valuable for bonsai. Although the trees may be different from the Asiatic types, they still can be handsome additions to any setting.

Some concessions have to be made in the Western method of bonsai, but using our own types of plants and containers and growing the tree in a few rather than in ten years need not detract from the beauty of this art.

PRINCIPLES OF BONSAI
Authentic bonsai trees have a natural weathered look, and they are viewed from all sides. Generally, plants of small stature and picturesque growth should be used; trees with small leaves, twigs, and branches are choice subjects. However, almost any woody plant

BONSAI CONTAINERS

—tree, shrub, or vine with a trunk and stem—can be grown as bonsai in a pot for many years. Thus, with skillful pruning and trimming the plant can be permanently dwarfed.

Natural dwarf plants of slow growth are easier to work with than large plants. It is most important that you choose a tree that has unusual characteristics—picturesque growth, handsome bark, irregular branches, low horizontal growth, or a stocky or twisted trunk.

The trunk is one vital part to consider in selecting a tree. Trees with straight trunks will be conical or rounded with horizontal branches and can be classed as formal. These trees are mainly coniferous evergreens (that is, they do not shed leaves). Informal upright trees have slightly curved trunks; the slanting trees have trunks that bend from the base to make a wider angle. There are also cascading trees whose trunks usually bend down sharply and extend below the edge of the container, and multiple-trunked trees are other possibilities. Surface roots can also be an asset, for they add a horizontal effect and create an illusion of age. All these many variations in tree growth suggest a certain attitude and character.

The tree is the main consideration in bonsai, but the container is vital too. It must fit the plant, for it is like a picture frame; it must be in character with the whole composition—neither too wide, high, garish, nor ornate for the tree. Remember that although the tree is the center of interest, the container shows it off.

Japanese bonsai pots, shallow bowls of glazed or unglazed ceramic, come in many sizes, shapes, colors, and textures (they are never glazed on the inside). Select containers of muted earth tones, for they complement most plants. Blue, green, or gray containers are handsome for brightly colored deciduous plants. Black and white containers are ideal for almost all plants. Remember that an upright bonsai looks best in a rectangular bowl, and slanting trees are handsome in either round or square pots. Round or octagonal dishes suit the cascading bonsai. These are suggestions, not rules, because every tree has its own character, which will dictate the type of pot to use.

PLANTING AND TRAINING

There are no set pruning rules; pruning depends on the tree and the attitude you are trying to achieve. In general, all excess growth that detracts from the tree should be removed, allowing only a few branches of the tree to establish the character. Shorten overlong branches and branches that are opposite each other. Branches that cross unattractively or go in the wrong direction also can be eliminated. After removing unnecessary branches, study the basic form of the tree to decide what other pruning is needed. Does it need more space to reveal the form of the tree or trunk?

To shape the tree to its final design, wire the trunk and branches and bend them into the desired position. Be gentle and ease up if a branch shows signs of breaking. Use copper wire (available at nurseries), insert it deeply in the soil or through the drainage hole, and coil it around the branches that are being trained. Do not wrap the wire around the branches too tightly, as it can injure the tree. Leave the wires on until the limbs develop; this may be six months to a year or more, depending on the tree.

Often a second wiring is necessary to really achieve the design, but let the tree rest a while before this second training. You can also train trees by tying branches with string or by placing lead weights (available at suppliers) at the tips of branches. After the tree has been shaped, cut back the roots. (Plants are root pruned to keep roots near the surface of the soil.) To prune the roots, place a pencil through the root system and remove old soil. Trim the root stems back and repot, but do not water too much for the first few weeks.

To pot the small tree, cover the drainage holes in the container with a mesh screen and over this sift a thin layer of finely crushed gravel. Put in a layer of somewhat coarse soil, followed by a layer of medium coarse soil. Now dig a depression in the soil to accommodate the roots of the tree. Settle the tree in place with a twisting motion and pack soil around the roots, tamping down to eliminate any air pockets. Cover the top of the soil with some fine moss to prevent soil washing out when you water the bonsai. Soak the container by standing it in water to the rim, and then water the tree sparingly for a few weeks until it is established.

Potting soil for most dwarf trees and shrubs should be one part garden soil, one part humus, and one part coarse, rather sandy, clay soil. Some plants will need a heavier structured (more loam) soil, but this depends on individual plants. Be sure the soil drains well, but still holds a certain amount of moisture.

I do not have set times for repotting plants. Instead, I watch how

(MUGO PINE)

1. Study the tree thoroughly to learn it's structure.

2. Determine as clearly as possible how the tree is to be trained.

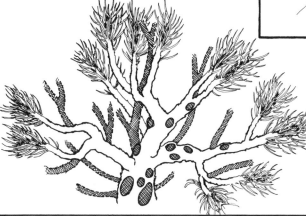

3. Prune out all branches definitely unnecessary for final shaping.

4. Bend branches into final form using copper wire anchored in soil at the base of tree.

HOW TO TRAIN A BONSAI

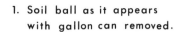

1. Soil ball as it appears with gallon can removed.

2. Gently break away soil leaving some intact at base of trunk.

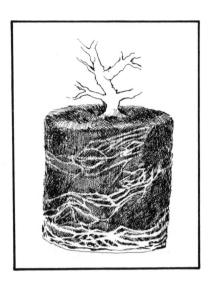

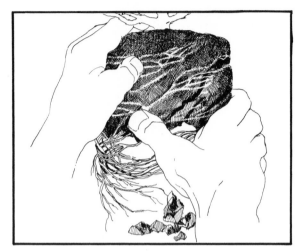

3. Prune roots in relation to size of the pruned tree and the container.

4. Cover holes in container with screen and insert wires to use for securing tree in place.

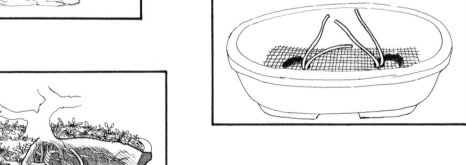

5. Once in place, sift and pack soil under and around roots. Top with ground cover ; water .

Hoeppner

HOW TO PLANT A BONSAI

Begonia dregei is grown in bonsai style in this handsome container. Note that the plant is placed to the right with small stones at the left to balance the arrangement. Photo by Joyce R. Wilson.

a plant grows; if after a year it stops growing, I generally repot in fresh soil. On the other hand, if after two years it is still thriving, it remains in the pot. I repot evergreens every third year.

CARE

In restricted space and soil, bonsai plants dry out quickly, and even though other plants can withstand drought for a few days, bonsai cannot. Generally they need water every day in spring and summer, preferably in the morning. Lingering moisture can cause leaf stains in some species. I use a fine-nozzle watering can, but a fog nozzle is a good substitute. Just remember not to dislodge soil with a strong blast of water.

In winter less moisture is needed, but do not let the soil get bone dry. Give bonsai an outdoor location with free air ventilation, but away from drafts that will harm plants. A good place is under a tree that allows plenty of light to filter through and yet provides some protection from direct noon sunlight. Tables or benches can be used to hold bonsai, or concrete blocks can be placed to accommodate the plants. The main consideration is that plants be at waist level so that it is easy to tend and to see them.

Standard plants can tolerate and generally need feedings, but a bonsai, although it too needs nutrients, should be fed in small doses.

A small Ficus *is perfect for bonsai growing; this one is indeed handsome in a pottery container.* Photo by Roche.

Too much food makes it grow too large; too little food will produce weak growth. I use a very weak solution of Hyponex or Miracle-Gro in spring, summer, and fall—one application per month. When fertilizing plants, observe these rules:

1. Do not feed a newly rooted or repotted plant for several weeks.
2. Do not feed a weak or sick plant.
3. Do not feed a plant when soil is dry in containers.
4. Do not feed when in doubt.

The proper winter care of trees will vary with the geographical area. In cold winters plants must be protected. I put mine in a cool garden room, but they can also be wintered successfully in a cool, but not freezing, greenhouse or unheated garage. Remember to keep soil somewhat moist; even deciduous plants, such as elm and maple, cannot be carried bone dry through winter.

A cool period is necessary for good health for most bonsai trees, so don't put them in warmth under any circumstances. For the most part, bonsai must be grown outdoors, as they do not do well inside all year.

Material for bonsai can be purchased from nursery suppliers, florists, or bonsai specialists. True dwarf plants or small house plants can be used, too.

This small begonia with gnarled growth makes an excellent bonsai subject. Photo by Joyce R. Wilson.

Plants for Bonsai (Trees, Shrubs):

Acer palmatum—Japanese maple
Cotoneaster horizontalis—cotoneaster
Cryptomeria japonica var. *nana*
Juniperus procumbens—juniper
Pinus mugo—mugo pine
Rhododendron obtusum—kurume azalea

Native Plants for Bonsai (Seedlings):

Betula lenta—sweet birch
Celastrus scandens—bittersweet
Fagus grandifolia—American beech
Ilex verticillata—winterberry
Juniperus virginiana—Eastern red-cedar
Kalmia latifolia—mountain laurel
Tsuga canadensis—hemlock
Vaccinium angustifolium—blueberry

House Plants for Bonsai:

If you are restricted to indoor growing, try some of these commonly available house plants.

Begonia dregei
B. foliosa
B. "Lulandi"
Carissa grandiflora—natal plum
Ficus diversifolia—mistletoe
Gardenia
Hedera helix—English ivy
Malpighia coccigera—miniature holly
Pelargonium—geranium
Pittosporum tobira—Japanese pittosporum
Punica granatum var. *nana*—pomegranate

All citrus, especially dwarfs such as Meyer lemon and otaheite orange, can also be used.

5. Miniature Plants ✍

There are miniatures in many plant families, but roses, geraniums, orchids, and begonias are perhaps the most desirable. The small gems of the gesneriads family—African violets, columneas, strepto-carpus—are beautiful too, and the beauty of the diminutive has been well sculptured in cacti and succulents. What you choose depends on your own tastes, and there are enough small plants to keep you busy a lifetime. Some are more challenging than others and require some experience to grow to perfection, but others grow by them-selves. I have a collection of small orchids, cacti, and succulents that have traveled with me for many years from Illinois to Florida to California. (The tiny begonias and geraniums I had, I am sorry to say, could not withstand the rigors of travel.)

As mentioned, in a window that could accommodate a dozen standard-sized plants you can grow several dozen different minia-ture ones—orchids, begonias, and roses. And a window is a spot to learn, see, and appreciate plants you otherwise could not grow in limited spaces.

ROSES
These fine flowers are universally admired because of their intri-cately shaped blossoms that unfurl into sheer loveliness. There are hundreds of hybrids, sometimes called fairy roses, that rarely grow more than fourteen inches tall and bloom indoors on and off through-out the year. The flowers may be as large as a quarter or as small as a dime and may be single, semidouble, or double in form.

Like their larger cousins, miniature roses need care. They like

Miniature roses are always desirable, whether in pots at windows or in tiny arrangements. Photo by Wayside Gardens.

coolness (55° to 65° F.) and as much sunshine as possible, especially in winter. (If you can't give them the bright light they need to bloom, it is senseless to grow them.) A moist but cool atmosphere is another requirement; place plants on moist gravel or mist them frequently. Remember to keep the soil evenly moist, never dry or soggy.

If you buy roses in spring and summer, they will be actively growing. In other seasons they may be dormant, with the stems cut back to about two inches, but they will start growth quickly and within a few months produce blooms. Whenever you buy roses, repot them in small containers with a fairly heavy potting mix.

If growing conditions are too hot and dry, there is a good chance red spider will attack plants. Leaves that develop white spots, eventually turn yellow, and fall off, indicate these insects; if plants are infested, cut them back to three inches, dust with a miticide, and grow in cooler and more moist conditions. If possible, summer roses

44

outdoors—a back porch or window box will do. They need little space and can be tucked into any outdoor nook.

Rose Varieties:

New varieties are introduced yearly; these are only some suggestions:

"Baby Gold Star"—a bushy miniature with double, golden yellow flowers

"Bo-Peep"—full double pink flowers; needs sun and light

"Cinderella"—double white blooms touched with pink in cool climates

"Dian"—double fragrant flowers of light red; needs careful pruning

"Easter Morning"—double flowers of pure ivory white

"Lilac Time"—lilac pink buds with pure lilac blooms

"Little Buckaroo"—bright red flowers with glossy foliage

"Lollipop"—vivid red flowers

"Mary Haywood"—a dense, compact bush with double pink flowers

"Midget"—fragrant, deep rose, three-fourth-inch blooms

"Mr. Bluebird"—large semidouble flowers of an unusual lavender blue

"Pink Heather"—floriferous, with tiny double pink flowers

"Pixie"—considered the smallest, completely double, white miniature rose

"Pixie Gold"—excellent miniature rose; golden yellow

"Pixie Rose"—excellent miniature rose; a bright shade of rose

"Red Imp"—small bright crimson blooms

"Robin"—perfectly shaped buds with quilled petals of deep red

"Sparkie"—bright red flowers with glossy dark foliage

"Sweet Fairy"—loose pink flowers

"Tinker Bell"—bright pink flowers with many petals

"Westmont"—double cherry red flowers

ORCHIDS

Here are the diminutive gems of the orchid world, and finer plants are difficult to find. Whether on a windowsill or a coffee table, in a miniature greenhouse, or on the kitchen counter, orchids offer a wealth of color for little effort.

Miniature orchid on driftwood: Platyclinis species. Photo by author.

Although the plants are small, the flowers are not insignificant; many miniatures produce blooms three inches across on a three-inch plant! Others may have a series of small flowers shaped to form an oval or ellipse, with tiny blossoms in exquisite star shapes and spheres of color. And some species have flowers so small that they must be viewed through a magnifying glass to be truly appreciated.

It will take miniature orchids a longer time to adjust to their new conditions than their larger relatives. They can be temperamental, but, once established, they need little care—perhaps less attention than most house plants. At first water them sparingly; too often people flood them to get them to grow, which can be fatal. Wait a few weeks or even a month until you see signs of new growth before you give them regular moisture.

Miniature orchids are sold in thumbnail pots or on pieces of tree fern or rafts. Plants on bark hanging from rafters or ceilings are

46

decorative, but they are difficult to water and dry out so quickly that often they can get bone dry in a hot summer day. Put a number of plants that require the same conditions in a large pot to minimize the danger of rapid drying out; then watering is easy.

To pot small orchids, use fir bark (fine grade) or osmunda. Put drainage materials into the pot and fill one-third of it with bark or osmunda. Place plants in the center and fill the pot with planting material. Press the fiber toward the center of the pot; most miniatures require tight potting. Some orchids will need bright sun, but most will prosper with only bright light. All will grow in average home temperatures of 72°F. by day and 62°F. at night.

To ensure bloom, observe the rest periods of orchids, which generally occur after or before flowering. It is difficult to carry plants bone dry for several weeks, but you must with orchids if they are to bloom again the following year.

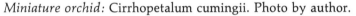

Miniature orchid: Cirrhopetalum cumingii. Photo by author.

This miniature oncidium *orchid grows on a tree fern slab.* Photo courtesy of American Orchid Society.

Orchids:

Angraecum compactum—three-inch white flowers and dark green straplike leaves

Asocentrum ampullaceum—dark green leaves and erect spikes of cerise flowers

A. miniatum—spikes of orange blooms with straplike dark green foliage

Capanemia uliginosa—small scented white flowers and solitary cactus-like fleshy leaves

Cattleya walkeriana—leathery green leaves and three-inch rose-colored flowers

Epidendrum lindleyanum—leafy stems and lavender flowers in autumn

E. polybulbon—leaves on a creeping rhizome and brownish yellow flowers with white heart-shaped lip

E. porpax—tiny oval green leaves and waxy brownish purple flowers

Kerfersteinia gramineus—one-inch yellowish green flowers with brownish red spots

Leptotes bicolor—succulent foliage and large white-stained, deep violet flowers

Masdevallia lilliputana—rarely taller than one inch; red and yellow flowers

M. schroederiana—dark green foliage and helmet-shaped deep red flowers with spurs

Notylia longispicata—small plant with large white blooms

Odontoglossum krameri—handsome white flowers with yellow center

Ornithocephalus bicornis—leathery leaves in rosette growth and bell-shaped greenish white blooms; best grown on raft

Orthochilus fuscus—leathery pendant leaves and small bearded yellow and red blooms; best grown on raft

P. chinensis—creamy white flowers, evenly spaced on a pendant stem; best grown on raft

Dendrobium jenkinsii, *a lovely miniature orchid crowned with flowers.* Photo courtesy of American Orchid Society.

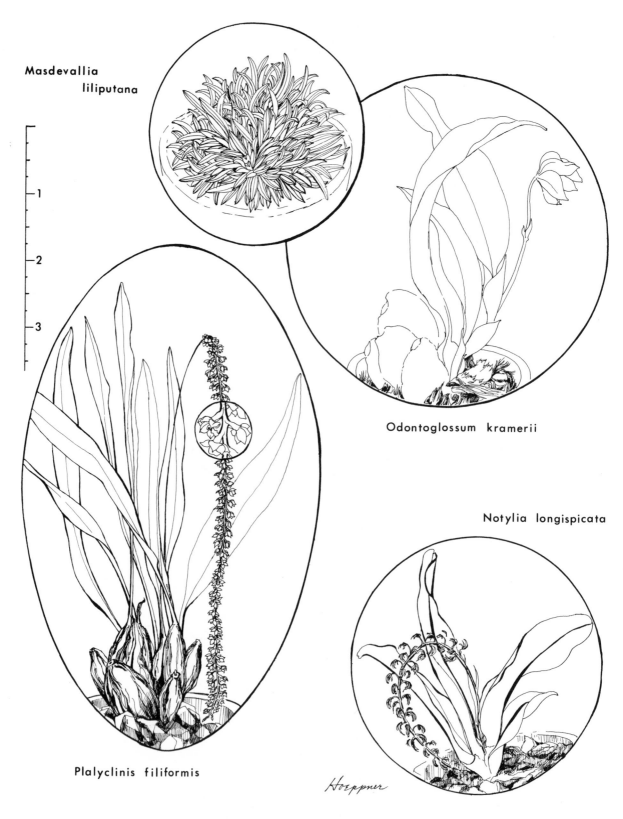

Masdevallia
liliputana

1

2

3

Odontoglossum kramerii

Notylia longispicata

Plalyclinis filiformis

Hoeppner

MINIATURE ORCHIDS

Pholidota articulata—cascading flower spike with one-half-inch yellow white flowers

Platyclinis cornuta—solitary leaves and white flowers on a short scape; best grown on raft

P. filiformis (also known as *Dendrochilum filiforme*)—grassy foliage and tiny yellow flowers

Pleurothallis aribuloides—spatula dark green leaves and very brilliant burnt-orange bloom

P. ghiesbreghtiana—long pendant stems of lemon yellow flowers in winter

Stelis ciliaris—tongue-shaped dark green leaves and tiny red blooms

S. micrantha—tiny greenish white flowers and six-inch green foliage

Geraniums (Pelargonium)

Dwarf and miniature geraniums are just as showy as their larger relatives, and they are easy to grow in bright light or under artificial light. Keep soil evenly moist and provide a place with good air circulation; do not feed them too much—perhaps once every third watering. Use three- to four-inch pots; smaller containers dry out too quickly. Give them a soil mixture with plenty of sand, so that drainage is almost perfect. There are plain- and fancy-leaved dwarfs and miniatures with single or double flowers. Do not fret if geraniums don't fare too well when you receive them, because it takes a while for these plants to adjust to new conditions.

Geranium Varieties:

"Aldebaran"—small dark green leaves marked with black green and pink flowers

"Allair"—intense green foliage and pink blooms

"Bumble Bee"—dark green leaves and red flowers

"Capella"—forest-green zonale foliage and pink blooms

"Emma Horsley"—double flowers, light pink with white

"Etna"—a fine red

"Fairy Princess"—dark leaves and creamy pink blooms

"Firefly"—dark green foliage and double red flowers

"Fleurette'—startling dark green leaves and salmon flowers

"Gypsy Gem"—small dark green leaves and double red flowers

Miniature geraniums are colorful and bright, most of them easy to grow indoors.
Photos by Merry Gardens.

"Imp"—dark foliage and salmon-pink flowers
Kliener Leibling "Green Gold"—dazzling green
Kliener Leibling *Variegata*—handsome variegated foliage
"Lilliput Lemon"—lemon-scented waxy leaves
"Moonbeam"—dark-zoned foliage and orange blooms
"North Star"—white with pink veins; good accent plant
"Polaris"—dark green foliage and white pink-edged flowers
"Robin Hood"—cherry-red double blooms
"Salmon Comet"—black green leaves and salmon blooms
"Snow Baby"—pure white blossoms
"Sparkle"—dark foliage and red flowers
"Tangerine"—free-blooming salmon
"Tweedledee"—scalloped leaves and salmon blooms

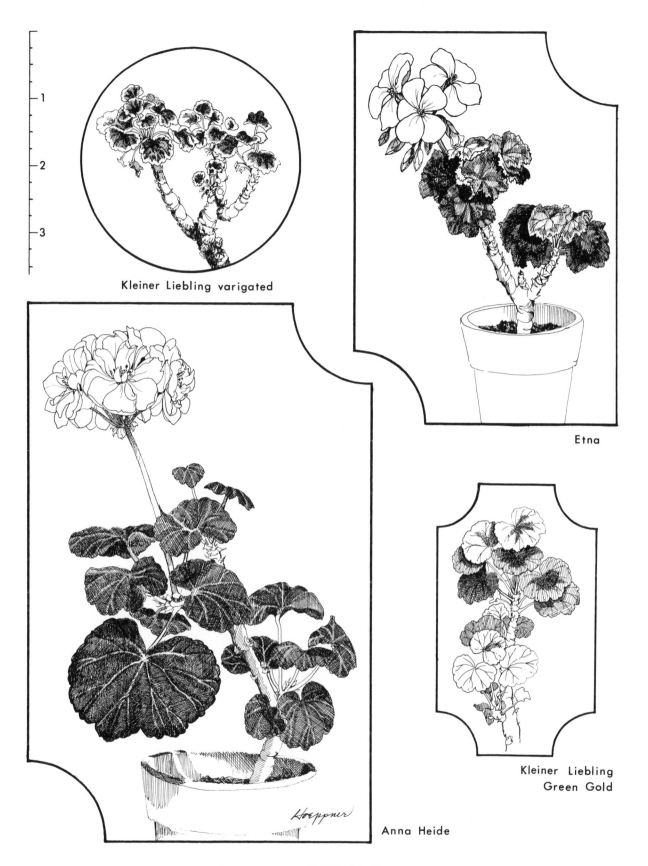

1

2

3

Kleiner Liebling varigated

Etna

Anna Heide

Hoeppner

Kleiner Liebling
Green Gold

DWARF GERANIUMS

BEGONIAS

Begonias come in an assortment of shapes, sizes, foliages, and flowers. Suppliers usually classify them as hairy leaved, rhizomatous, angel wing, wax, and rex types, and within each group there are some small species. With such a variety, cultivation differs from one plant to the next, so begonias do take care. Do not be misled into thinking they will thrive by themselves.

Perhaps the easiest to manage indoors are the rhizomatous types with their picturesque gnarled growth and ornamental round or star-shaped leaves in plain or fancy patterns. This stemlike root stores up food and moisture, so, if you forget to water the plants for a few days, they still flourish. In fact, allow the soil to dry out thoroughly between waterings. Most varieties are shallow-rooted, so avoid deep pots or the soil will turn sour from too much water and injure the plants. Use a light humusy soil and never bury the rhizomes. Give plants bright light with as much sun as possible in winter.

For years wax begonias (*Begonia semperflorens*) have been popular because of their bright tiny flowers and glossy dark green or mahogany leaves. Use small pots for these charmers and give them a bright place. They like to be quite dry; too much water rots them quickly. Prune back tops as plants get leggy. Wax begonias are nice plants for arrangements and color accents.

Rex begonias are mostly rhizomatous, and some of the miniatures, with their exquisite patterned leaves, are well worth having. The plants thrive on neglect; the more attention I give mine, the less they seem to grow. The secret seems to be to put them in a somewhat cool (68°F.) moist, shady place and water them only a few times a week. In sun they rarely succeed, and with too much water at the roots they invariably die. Most types drop their leaves and go dormant in winter, so don't try to force them to grow then. Water sparingly and wait for new growth; then resume watering.

Begonias:

B. albo-picta—small green silver-spotted leaves and dark pink blossoms

"Baby Perfectifolia"—deep green and shiny pointed leaves with chocolate-laced edge

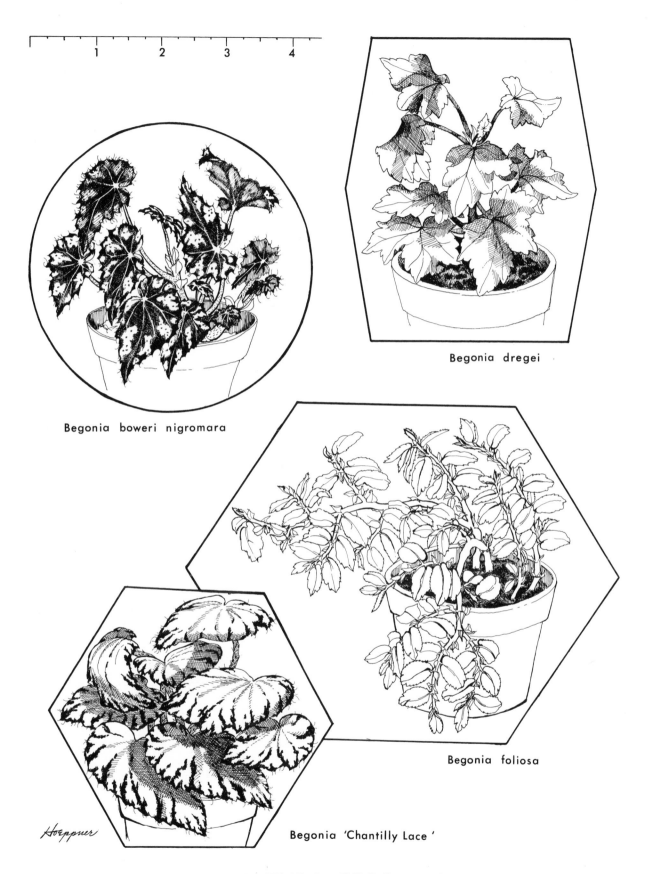

Begonia dregei

Begonia boweri nigromara

Begonia foliosa

Begonia 'Chantilly Lace'

MINIATURE BEGONIAS

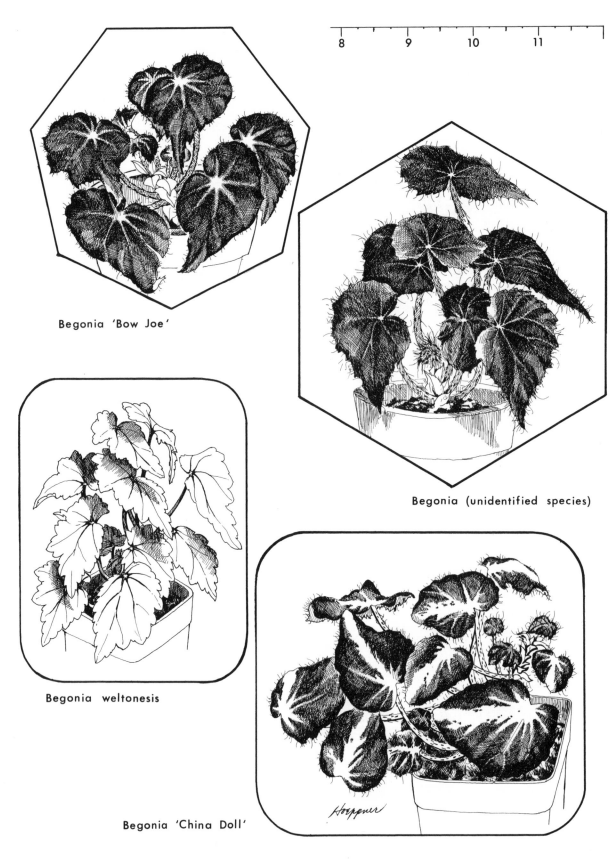

Begonia 'Bow Joe'

Begonia (unidentified species)

Begonia weltonesis

Begonia 'China Doll'

MINIATURE BEGONIAS

"Baby Rainbow"—green leaves with a purple center and a purplish brown margin suffused with carmine-red; silver spotted

Begonia dregei—succulent red stems and thin leaves that are shallow lobed, bronzy green with purple veins; white flowers

B. foliosa—a dainty and fernlike with drooping branches clothed in tiny oblong leaves; showers of white flowers

B. imperialis var. *smaragdina*—light green emerald leaves that are velvet and pebble textured; white flowers

Begonia richardsiana—green maple, red sinus and underleaf; white flowers

B. weltoniensis—somewhat large, but handsome foliage

"Berry Autumn"—reddish brown center and edge, inner zone olive green and faintly dotted silver

"Black Falcon"—black star-shaped leaves with wide silver marking outlining the veins; clusters of pink flowers

"Bow Chance"—dark green leaves with light green sinus and veins; reddish brown stems and pink flowers

"Bow Joe"—one of the daintiest; tiny black pointed leaves with light green sinus and clusters of pink flowers

"Chantilly Lace"—chartreuse leaves with black edges

"China Doll"—small, light green and pointed leaves with wide brown veins and hairy edges; clusters of small pink flowers

"It"—light green leaves with silver dots and pink flowers

"Little Gem"—pygmy plant with reddish brown leaves and ruffled double pink flowers

"Lucy Closson"—small dark leaves flecked with silver and rose

"Mazie"—round bronzy green satin leaves and pink flowers

"Midget"—small star-shaped black leaves and pink flowers

"Pansy"—lobed metallic green leaves with center star of dark green

"Pistachio"—small green leaves; pink flowers with thimblelike green center, changing to pink as they open

"Red Berry"—reddish brown leaves with autumn hues

"Rosa Kugel"—small green cupped leaves and pink flowers; compact

"Spaulding"—brownish green upper leaf and red under leaf with hairy margin; pink flowers

"Virbob"—star-shaped leaves marbled in green, chartreuse, bronze, and deep red; pink flowers

"Zee Bowman"—pointed green leaves marbled silver; pink flowers

Miniature succulents, such as Haworthias, make ideal house plants and almost grow by themselves. Photo by Joyce R. Wilson.

Cacti and Succulents

With 1,300 species distributed among 200 genera, the cactus family is huge. Most cacti are succulents, but not all succulents are cacti, and the nomenclature tends to be confusing because taxonomists are frequently taking a plant from one group and putting it into another. Cacti and succulents include some of the most rewarding plants for home culture, since they can grow under adverse conditions—drought, dry atmosphere—if necessary. Many are small plants, making them ideal for windowsill growing. Although most are desert plants, some, like the orchid cactus and christmas cactus, are from tropical forests. Cacti store water in their thickened stems, which eliminates the need for leaves; succulents use their fleshy leaves as water reservoirs.

Many of the succulents, especially cacti, must be grown dry *and* cool during their winter rest. Both types require a sandy soil; I use equal parts of sand and loam. If you want your cacti and succulents to live for years, water them with care. Although most prefer to be dry, the soil should never be allowed to become powdery. In the warm months most can take a great deal of water. Grow the plants at a sunny window in winter; the rest of the year they prosper at a western or eastern exposure.

Cacti And Succulents:
  Crassula—to eight inches
C. *cooperii*—small pointed leaves with dark markings
C. *schmidtii*—pointed red-tinted leaves
  Echinocactus—young plants to sixteen inches
E. *grusonii*—golden yellow globe and yellow blooms
E. *horizonthalonius*—silver gray and pink leaves with red spines
  Echinocereus (hedgehog cactus)—to twelve inches; many varieties
E. *dasyacanthus*—small dense spines and yellow flowers
E. *pentalophus*—fingerlike stems and red blooms
E. *reichenbachii*—ribbed globe and white to red brown flowers
E. *rigidissimus*—multicolored spines of pink, white, red, and brown
  Echinopsos (sea-urchin cactus)—four to sixteen inches
E. *campylacantha*—grayish green globe and purple white blooms
E. *eyriesii*—brown spines and white flowers
E. *multiplex*—dark green barrel shape with rose flowers
  Faucaria (tiger jaws)—to twelve inches
F. *bosscheana*—glossy green leaves and yellow flowers
F. *tigrina*—gray green plant with large yellow blooms
  Gymnocalycium (chin cactus)—to ten inches
G. *mihanovichii*—gray green globe and white flowers
G. *quehlianum*—white and red blooms
G. *schickendantzii*—white or pinkish white flowers
  Haworthia—to twenty inches
H. *margaritifera*—pointed leaves with white warts
H. *viscosa*—low rosette with pale green foliage
  Kalanchoë—to twenty inches
K. *blossfeldiana*—red Christmas blooms
K. *carnea*—pink species
  Kleinia (candle plant)—to twenty-four inches
K. *articulata*—bluish leaves and white flowers
K. *pendula*—large scarlet blooms
  Lobivia (cob cactus)—to fourteen inches
L. *aurea*—yellow
L. *backebergii*—red
L. *famatimensis*—orange
  Rebutia (crown cactus)—four to fifteen inches
R. *kupperiana*—scarlet flowers

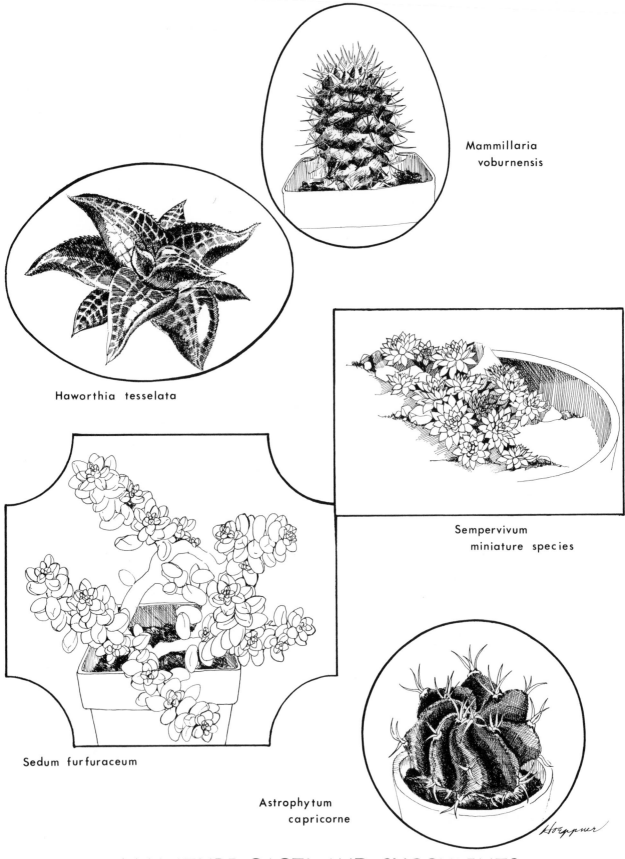

Mammillaria
voburnensis

Haworthia tesselata

Sempervivum
miniature species

Sedum furfuraceum

Astrophytum
capricorne

MINIATURE CACTI AND SUCCULENTS

R. minuscula—scarlet blooms

R. violaciflora—purple flowers

Sedum—to eight inches

S. adolphii—yellow green bushy growth and white flowers

S. dasyphyllum—blue green rosette with pink blooms

S. furfuraceum—tiny jadelike emerald green leaves

S. lineare—needlelike leaves and bright yellow flowers

S. multiceps—shrubby growth and lovely yellow blooms

African Violets and Other Gesneriads

African violets are popular plants and deservedly so, for they offer a wealth of color indoors. There are many fine new miniatures of improved form that make perfect house plants, and in the same family there are other ideal plants that have been completely over-looked and yet are as striking in bloom as the violets.

Columneas, kohlerias, episcias, and streptocarpus are all fine house plants that do not require excessive light or too much care, and *Sinningia pusilla*, the miniature gloxinia, is perhaps one of the finest miniatures. Many of these plants, formerly scarce, are now available from suppliers and should certainly be grown more.

Rebutias are fine miniature cacti that bear handsome bright colorful flowers. Photo by Joyce R. Wilson.

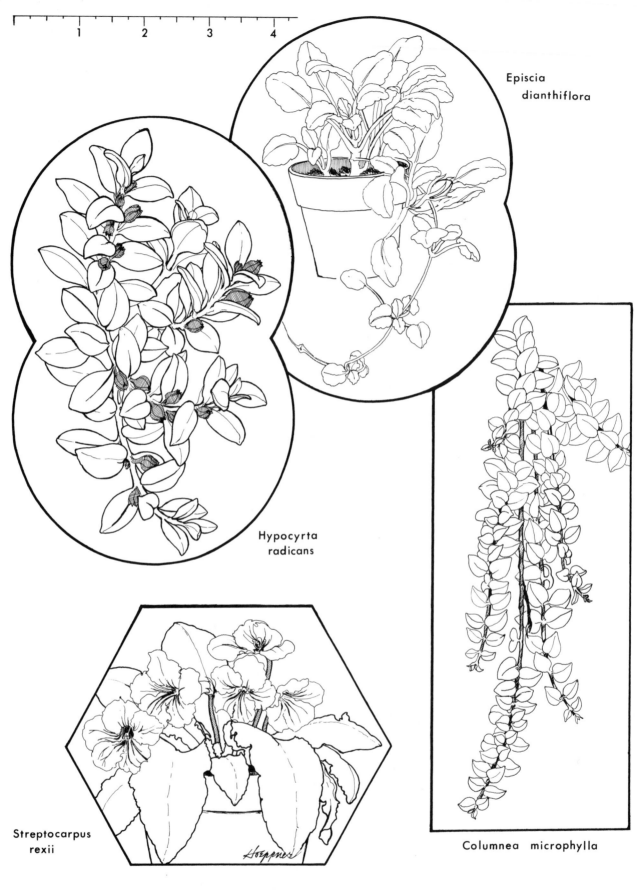

Episcia
dianthiflora

Hypocyrta
radicans

Columnea microphylla

Streptocarpus
rexii

GESNERIADS

African Violet Varieties:

"Bonanza"—ruffled red violet flowers
"Carita"—fine blue blooms
"Fancy Doll"—dark pink and white blossoms
"Irish Elf"—frilled double white flowers
"Little Mo"—bronzy red violet foliage with green edges
"Miniken"—double blue and white flowers

Other Gesneriads:

Columnea microphylla—tiny, hairy, coppery leaves and red flowers
Episcia dianthiflora—dark green leaves and white flowers
Hypocyrta nummularia—red hairy stems and small orange yellow
  flowers
H. radicans—shiny green leaves and orange yellow blooms
Kohleria amabilis—bell-shaped white flowers with purple throat
Sinningia pusilla—orchid color with darker veins and yellow throat;
S. "Dolly Baby"—another excellent choice
Streptocarpus rexii—lovely blue or mauve flowers
S. saxorum—pale lilac flowers with white throat

6. Miniature Flower Arrangements ✐

When you start making miniature flower arrangements you really see and appreciate nature at work; every tiny flower, twig, and seed pod takes on new interest and meaning. If you think you know plants, a new experience awaits you when you start using them in miniature arrangements. With a little imagination even the novice can create arrangements that have dozens of uses; on a coffee table or window-sill, in niches or nooks, or in a bathroom or bedroom, they are always a bright spot of color, delighting the eye and charming the viewer. The skilful use of miniature materials is easy to master, but it requires practice and time. Do not be discouraged if first arrangements

This arrangement in a Japanese saki cup, only two inches in diameter, features Oregon grape (top and right), sweet anise (center), and Crassula falcata blossoms (bottom). Photo by author; arrangement by Richard Lucier.

are less than perfect for in time you will find your fingers busily fixing flowers and twigs in appealing designs.

There are many plants and plant parts for arrangements—seed pods and plant berries, branches and twigs. Fresh flower arrangements will add days of color to the home, and dried arrangements last for months.

What to Use

Nature provides all kinds of grasses, sedges, mosses, and seed pods to work with. The garden yields tiny flowers of dianthus or clumps of spirea and viburnum; lobelias and ageratum are other fine choices, and most charming are dwarf tulips and daffodils (see Chapter 10). House plants offer many tiny ferns, mosses, gesneriads, and orchid blossoms, and immature flower buds and young shoots of larger plants can also be used. The blossoms of many crassulas and echeverias are made up of clusters of small flowers that are ideal for arrangements. Even shrubs offer possibilities; cotoneaster twigs and buxus leaves blend in well with miniature designs. Lovely rock-garden plants offer a harvest of flowers and foliage for tiny arrangements; sempervivums and draba are just a few that can be used. Even herbs—thyme or rosemary—become handsome accents in arrangements.

Making the Arrangement

Finding a container for miniature arrangements is almost as much fun as putting plants together. Thimbles, bottlecaps, tea cups, perfume bottles, small pottery dishes, buttons, seashells, inkwells, glass tops of coffee pots, brass tubes, and hardware are all good choices. Thus, the world of tiny containers is almost as intriguing and endless as the plants themselves.

Even though it is easy to find the vase or whatever, it is not always easy to match it with the arrangement. This is the essence of successful arrangements: the container and plants must match, and they must belong to each other. For example, at a friend's house one night I saw a lovely bouquet of bright red flowers in a handsome brass bottle two inches high. The flowers came from the house plant *Crassula falcata*. I had grown the same plant and had observed the same tiny brick-red blooms, but I had never really seen them. Now, cut and placed in water, they were vitally important. The succulent family contains numerous plants that bear panicles of bright flowers that

A handsome tea strainer holds an arrangement of white marguerites, English ivy seed clusters, and Dianthus in bud. (A small glass vial is inserted in the strainer to hold water.) Photo by author; arrangement by Richard Lucier.

A three-inch dish holds a lovely arrangement of miniature roses, Raphiolepis, and ivy geraniums. Photo by author; arrangement by Richard Lucier.

A shell only a few inches across is used for this miniature arrangement of seeds of Japanese anemone, Hebe blossoms, and seed clusters of English ivy. Photo by author; arrangement by Richard Lucier.

Dried arrangements with miniature plant materials are handsome too; this three-inch ceramic dish holds bearded oats (top), wild sweet pea (left), oriental poppy pods (right), and dried hydrangea. Photo by author; arrangement by Richard Lucier.

are ideal for small decorative designs, and the scarlet red blooms of *Rochea coccinea* make a breathtaking bouquet in a tiny white vase.

Design

Making flower arrangements takes experience; it is not something you will master overnight or even in a year. You can learn a great deal by observing pictures and following some basic rules of design, but the actual creation depends on you and your imagination and on practice, analysis, and more practice.

Scale is important in all flower arrangements and more so in miniature ones; a flower that is too large or too small for its design and its container ruins the whole effect. In large arrangements there is generally some room for error, but this is not so in small ones. Each piece —flower, twig, leaf, and accessory—must belong and be in scale to other elements in the total scene.

There are vertical, horizontal, and cascading arrangements. The character of the arrangement may be bold, fragile, traditional, or abstract. There are numerous variations to be governed only by your own imagination. For further reading consult a few good books on general design in flower arranging.

7. *Miniature Plants in the Landscape*

In a quiet, tucked-away place or a secluded corner of your property, a garden of miniature plants can be charming. Whether a flower bed, a border, or an island of color, this garden is unexpected beauty that delights the eye.

A miniature garden cannot replace a standard garden, but it can still bring texture and color to any given area. Many small annuals and perennials, bulbs, slow-growing evergreens, and shrubs are available for diminutive gardens. Small plants are better appreciated in a place of their own rather than with large plants, where they may be lost and out of scale. With small gardens maintenance is slight, and, once plants are established, they grow on their own with little further care.

There are many places where small plants can be used effectively. Take advantage of a natural breezeway area by turning it into an appealing garden or use the space at a back door for an attractive display of small plants.

Small Flower Garden

Even though this is a tiny garden, its beauty still depends on the requirements of all good gardens—scale, composition, and balance. Use masses of plants to avoid a spotty effect. Give annuals and perennials a frame of dwarf shrubs or evergreens. Stones for stability are useful, as are creeping ground covers such as chamomile and baby's tears.

Because my back yard is a sunny place I have used a combination of diminutive annuals, perennials, and bulbs interspersed with ground covers and accented with dwarf evergreens—round shapes where needed and vertical accents in other locations. There is a wind-

Petunias and alyssum combine to create a stunning small garden. Photo by George G. Ball.

"Elfin" impatiens are popular garden flowers and have many uses in the land-scape. Photo courtesy of Pan American Seed Company.

ing woodblock path and broad strokes of white gravel laced between the plants to provide contrast and to pull the scene together. It is a minimum maintenance garden that requires little care, but looks handsome all year.

Annuals and perennials need a good rich soil and almost perfect drainage to thrive. Select your plants according to their cultural needs. Most varieties need sun and an evenly moist neutral soil. Mix organic matter, such as leaf mold or compost, into the existing soil. The soil should not be sandy or heavy, but rather porous in texture and rich black in color. (Some plants will tolerate soggy conditions, but annuals and perennials will soon die, so make sure water drains readily from the soil.)

Most miniatures are shallow-rooted and can be harmed if the soil remains too dry too long, so provide adequate water often and deeply. (In fall, thorough watering often means the difference between winter survival and winter kill.) The plants' hardiness must also be considered, but this is not too important a factor if you buy from local nurseries. Some perennials do not thrive in hot summers, but others will.

Alternate freezing and thawing will heave plants from the soil, and, if there is no snow cover, plants will suffer greatly. When the ground is frozen, cover perennials with a light blanket of evergreen boughs or salt hay; remove this protective mulch a little at a time in early spring.

PERENNIALS

Botanical Name	Common Name	Height	Flower Color
Achillea tomentosa var. *nana*	wooly yarrow	4″	yellow
Adonis amurensis	pheasant's eye	12″	yellow
Ajuga repens	carpet bugleweed	6″	purple
Anchusa myosotidiflora		12″	blue
Androsace lanuginosa	rock jasmine	2″	rose
Anemone pulsatilla	European pasqueflower	9″	purple
Antennaria dioica var. *rosea*	pussy's toes	2″	pink
Anthemis nobilis	chamomile	10-12″	yellow
Aquilegia canadensis	common American columbine	18″	red and yellow
Arabis procurrens var. *nana*	rock cress	6-12″	white
Arenaria verna var. *caespitosa*	sandwort	2-4″	white
Armeria maritima	sea pink	6″	white to rose pink
Artemisia schmidtiana var. *nana*	silver mound wormwood	8″	foliage plant
Astilbe japonica	Japanese astilbe	12″	white, pink and red
Aubrieta deltoidea	common aubrieta	6″	purple
Bergenia cordifolia	heartleaf saxifragaceae	12″	rose
Campanula elatines var. *fenestrellata*	bellflower	3″	blue
Chrysanthemum ptarmicaeflorum		4-6″	silvery foliage
Dianthus deltoides	maiden pink	9″	pink
D. gratianopolitanus (*caesius*)	cheddar pink	3-12″	rose pink
D. plumarius	cottage pink	12″	various

Botanical Name	Common Name	Height	Flower Color
D. plumarius var. *Essexusten*		5″	rose pink
D. plumarius var. Her Majesty		4-6″	double white flowers
Dicentra cucullaria	Dutchman's breeches	10″	white
Gaillardia (dwarf)		8″	red and yellow
Geranium dalmaticum		4″	light pink
Helleborus niger	Christmas rose	12″	white
Iberis sempervirens	evergreen candytuft	12″	white
Iris (dwarf)		4-6″	many colors
Lithospermum prostratum (*diffusum*)		4-6″	deep blue
Lychnis viscaria	German catchfly	12″	purple
Mitella diphylla	bishop's cap	12″	white
Nepeta mussini	catmint	12″	blue
Nierembergia rivularis	white cup	2-4″	creamy white
Oenothera perennis	evening primrose	6″	yellow
Papaver nudicaule	Iceland poppy	12″	various
Phlox divaricata var. *canadensis*	wild sweet William	10″	lavender
Phlox subulata (many varieties)	ground pink	to 12″	pink, white and blue
Platycodon mariesi	balloon flower	12″	violet blue
Plumbago larpentiae	leadwort	6-8″	blue
Polygonum vaccinifolium	knotweed	5-6″	rose
Potentilla verna var. *nana*		2″	gold
Primula	primrose	9″	various
Pulmonaria angusti-folia	cowslip lungwort	12″	blue
Ranunculus repens	creeping buttercup	6″	yellow
Sanguinaria canadensis	bloodroot	8″	white

Botanical Name	Common Name	Height	Flower Color
Saxifraga aizoon var. rosea		3″	rose
Thymus serpyllum	mother-of-thyme		purplish
Veronica incana	wooly speedwell	12″	rose purple
V. spicata	spike speedwell	12″	purple
V. teucrium	rock speedwell	4″	blue
Viola cornuta	tufted pansy	8″	various
V. odorata	sweet violet	8″	violet

Dwarf asters are colorful garden flowers by themselves or with other flowers. Photo courtesy of Burpee Seed Company.

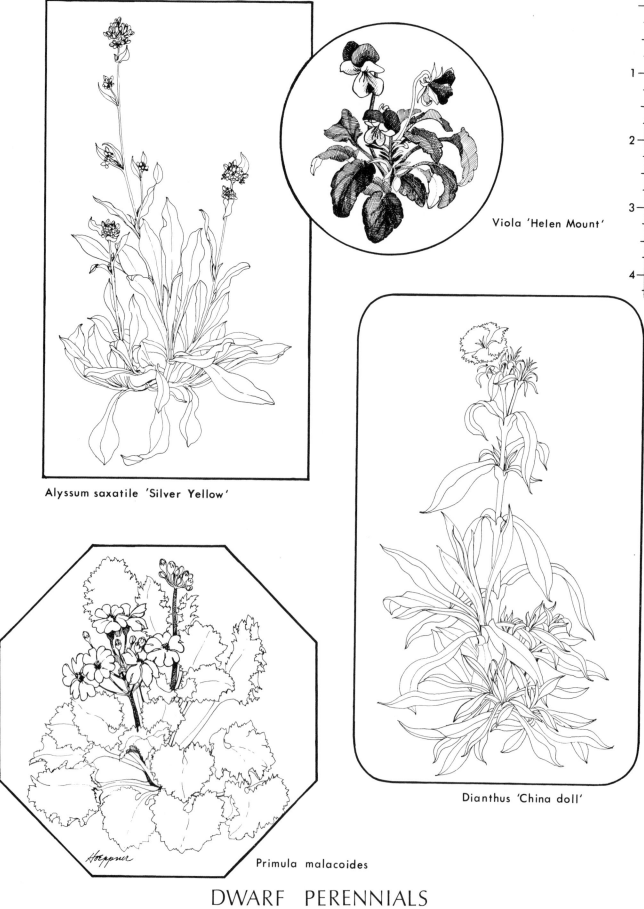

Viola 'Helen Mount'

Alyssum saxatile 'Silver Yellow'

Dianthus 'China doll'

Primula malacoides

DWARF PERENNIALS

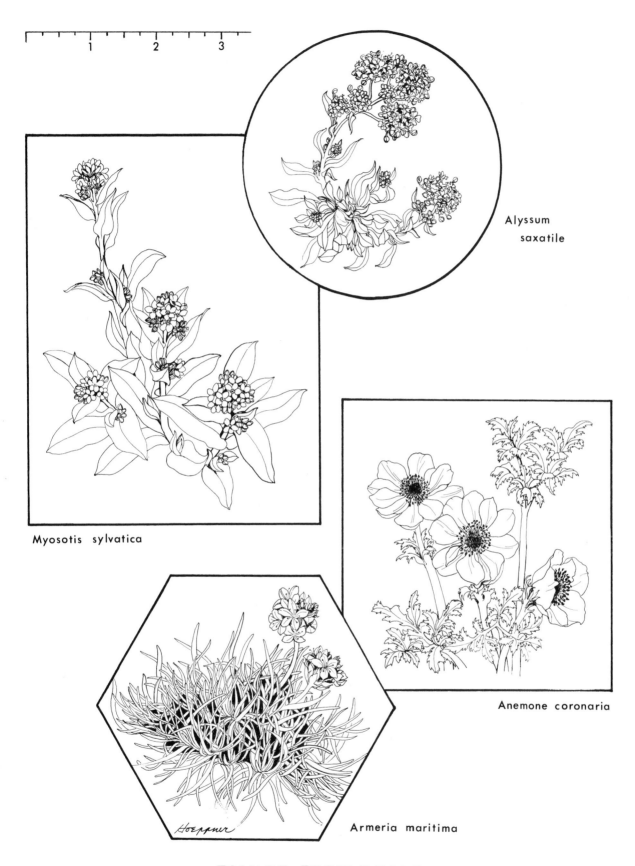

Alyssum
saxatile

Myosotis sylvatica

Anemone coronaria

Armeria maritima

Hoeppner

DWARF PERENNIALS

Ageratum
houstonianum

Lobularia maritima

Dahlia (dwarf) 'Sunburst'

Tagetes patula

DWARF ANNUALS

ANNUALS

Because annuals are usually recognized on sight, no descriptions are given. Instead, ask your nurseryman for the best varieties for your region. (New varieties of dwarf size are introduced yearly. For conifers and shrubs, see Chapter 8.)

Ageratum houstonianum (blue blazer)
A. "Blue Ball"
A. "Carpet of Snow"
Antirrhinum (dwarf varieties; snapdragon)
Centaurea cyanus (cornflower)
Coreopsis
Dahlia (dwarf varieties)
Impatiens (Elfin varieties)
Lathyrus (knee-hi sweet pea)
Lobularia maritima (sweet alyssum)
Petunia (dwarf varieties)
Phlox
Portulaca
Tagetes patula (marigold)
Tropaeolum (nasturtium)

Perennial houstonias are only three to six inches tall and are lovely in this rock setting. Photo by Roche.

8. Dwarf Conifer Trees, Evergreen Shrubs and Ground Covers ✐

Today's average property is small, and often dwarf trees and shrubs are in better scale in the landscape plan than large trees and shrubs. With them, even a ten by twenty feet piece of property can become a miniature verdant forest that is eye-catching and can bring special happiness to the gardener who cannot spare time or who does not have the energy to tend a large garden.

In dwarf conifers, evergreens, and shrubs you will find a storehouse of varying colors, forms, and textures, and working with these plants is not as demanding as landscaping with large standard shrubs and trees. It is far easier to judge the ultimate shape of a small tree than a large one, and, when you see a tiny shrub in seedling stage, you have a fairly good idea of what it will look like when mature. Furthermore, evergreens are low-maintenance plants that are green all year, and they seem to provide a better opportunity for choosing the proper tree shapes to use intelligently in the garden in order to produce a handsome, easy-to-care-for area. Narrow-leaved or cone-bearing evergreens, such as cypress and yew, are called conifers, which distinguishes them from such broad-leaved evergreens as rhododendron.

The size of small plants is frequently a topic at garden meetings because many suppliers list them as dwarf or pygmy or simply slow-growing. Just what is a Dwarf plant? To me, trees that are slow-growing, are dense in habit, or have a distinctive form different from the typical natural species are, in the broad sense, dwarf. Perhaps this is not technically correct, but there are just too many fine plants in this category to be overlooked. Also, growers are introducing fas-

Dwarf evergreen trees, frame a birdbath and are in perfect scale in the author's small garden. Photo by author.

cinating new small forms frequently, for properties are no longer vast. I prefer the dwarf plants for gardening because they are small and thus get small problems—nothing I cannot cope with.

A plant that grows as a dwarf in one area may not in another area because of degrees of soil fertility and geographical location. In a mild climate a plant will naturally grow taller than the same plant in a cold climate. And be aware of hardiness factors when working with dwarf evergreens. Cold tolerance is not the only measure of a plant's hardiness; the condition of the plant, soil moisture, length of freezing spells, and many other factors enter into the picture.

Most winter damage to evergreens is caused by drying winds and sunshine in periods of prolonged freezes, rather than from the cold itself. Snow cover helps greatly; otherwise other measures of protection must be observed.

Making the landscape plan with dwarf plants is a gardener's dream because there is a wealth of material, and the marriage of textures and the combination of forms is infinite. The small garden, like a large one, will depend on scale, balance, and harmony. But, as mentioned, unlike the large garden plan, for which it is difficult to predict what a plant will look like at maturity, dwarfs show their form even when young. This garden allows even the novice gardener to create a pleasing area. A few elementary design principles to observe follow:

1. Use round globe plants for mass; vertical ones as accents.
2. Avoid single plantings.
3. Use groups of the same species.
4. Know the color of the plant. Green is not simply green (especially with evergreens); it can be a dozen different hues.
5. Arrange the greens so they go from light to dark gradually or from dark to light without abrupt changes.
6. Avoid abrupt color changes.
7. Use texture in the design; there are infinite kinds.

Only general suggestions, rather than specific cultural rules, can be given for these plants, for success depends greatly on where and how they are grown. Generally, most of the following plants are easy to grow if given a moderately rich, well-drained soil that is neutral to slightly acid (pH 5 to 7). Most need some sun during the day, although Chamaecyparis and Cryptomerias do better in light shade.

For new gardens the dwarf conifers are indispensable in the design —they provide scale and accent. Some of the smaller shrubs mentioned later are also valuable in the new garden.

Dwarf Conifer Trees:

Abies balsamea var. *nana*—short, flat needles tightly arranged, forming a dense, ball-shaped bushlet

Chamaecyparis lawsoniana var. *forsteckensis*—blue green ball with branchlets twisted and clustered into cockscombs

C. lawsoniana var. *minima*—stiff fan-shaped dark green plumes, colored blue on underside

C. obtusa var. *coralliformis*—twisted branchlets resembling dark, emerald green coral

C. obtusa var. *lycopodioides*—deep green with blue; develops into a spreading bush

C. obtusa var. *nana gracilis*—dense fan-shaped branches; slow growing

C. pisifera var. *filifera nana*—pale green, long and thin threadlike branchlets

C. pisifera var. *plumosa minima*—curly, feathery branchlets; slow growing

C. pisifera var. *squarrosa aurea pygmaea*—light blue green with golden yellow; forms a dense ball-shaped plant

C. pisifera var. *squarrosa cyano viridis*—silvery blue green with soft, mossy foliage

Cryptomeria japonica var. *nana*—stiff and tiny needlelike leaves; slow growing

C. japonica var. *vilmoriniana*—stiff and tiny needlelike leaves; much smaller than *C. japonica* var. *nana*

Juniperus chinensis var. *pfitzeriana nana*—irregular spreading, slow-growing bushlet

J. chinensis var. *plumosa aurea*—golden-colored, vase-shaped low bush

J. communis var. *compressa*—light gray green foliage; slender columnar form

J. horizontalis var. *glomerata*—deep bright green; forms a dense rounded mound

J. squamata var. *meyeri*—bluish white with pink and purple in winter; dense and irregular upright growing

Picea abies var. *procumbens*—broad, flat-topped bushlet

P. glauca var. *conica*—light gray green leaves; dense, narrow conical form

P. abies var. *pumila*—dense, deep, dark green foliage

Taxus baccata var. *repandens* (spreading English yew)—horizontally spreading branches

T. cuspidata var. *minima*—tiny leaves and slow growing; very dwarf; dark green needles

Thuja occidentalis var. *minima*—light green color that turns bronzy in fall; small and very slow growing

T. occidentalis var. *ohlendorfii*—dark bluish green in color; bronzy in winter

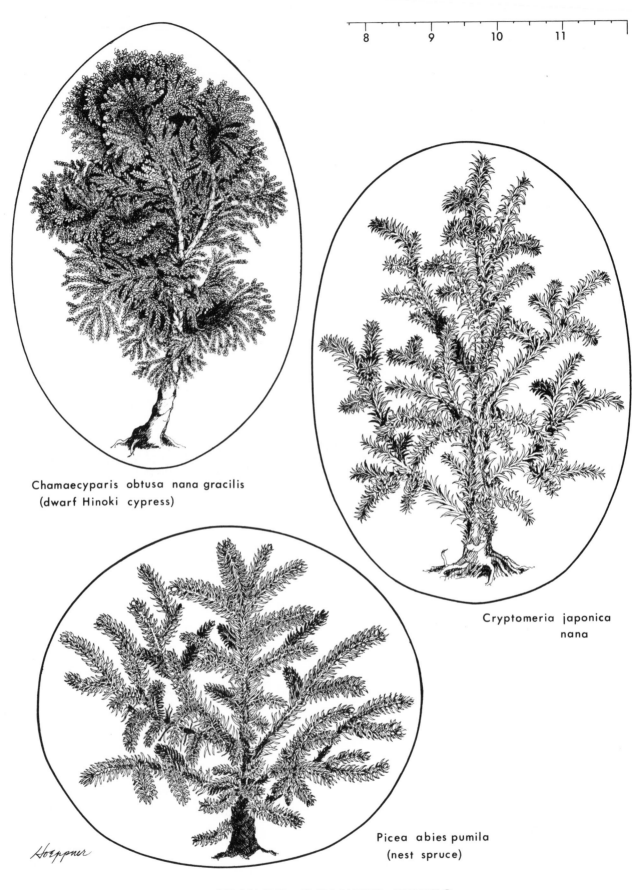

Chamaecyparis obtusa nana gracilis
(dwarf Hinoki cypress)

Cryptomeria japonica
nana

Picea abies pumila
(nest spruce)

Hoeppner

DWARF CONIFER TREES

Dwarf Evergreen Shrubs:

Andromeda polifolia var. *grandiflora compacta*—blue gray leathery leaves and large pink bells; low, spreading plant

A. polifolia var. *nana*—low, creeping plant; deep pink bells; red bronze in winter

Berberis buxifolia var. *nana*—compact shrub with dark reddish green leaves, large orange flowers

B. candidula—low, spreading hollylike leaves; large orange yellow flowers in spring; blackberries in late summer

B. stenophylla var. *nana compacta*—blue green spiny leaves; twiggy growth (needs protection)

Bruckenthalia spiculifolia (Balkan heath)—small pink bell-like flowers and sprucelike leaves

Buxus microphylla var. *koreana*—forms a dwarf rounded ball (can be sheared to any shape for formal edgings)

B. microphylla var. *nana compacta*—dwarf box with tiny leaves in a tight ball

Calluna vulgaris (many varieties)

Cotoneaster horizontalis var. "Little Gem"—short horizontal branches with shiny green leaves that turn crimson in fall

C. microphylla var. *cooperi*—textured tiny evergreen leaves; white flowers and red berries; slow growing

Daphne cneorum (garland flower)—dense arching stems with light leaves; clustering and fragrant pink flowers

Euonymus fortunei var. *minimus* (dwarf winter creeper)—fine small flowers in spring; evergreen tiny leaves

Forsythia viridissima var. *broxensis*—low, rounded bush with large yellow flowers in early spring; profuse bloomer

Hebe decumbens—tiny gray green leaves; short spikes of white flowers

Ilex crenata var. *helleri*—slow-growing Japanese holly; tiny leaves; sometimes classed as a tree

Pieris japonica var. *compacta*—dense evergreen bush with white lily-of-the-valley bells

P. japonica var. *variegata*—foliage edged with light yellow; new growth pink and crimson with subdued yellow; urn-shaped flowers in early spring; slow growing

Azalea 'Gumpo'

Ilex cornuta

Pieris japonica compacta

Hoeppner

DWARF SHRUBS

Rhododendron fastigiatum—blue green leaves; deep purple flowers in late April

R. "Gumpo"—dense, low-growing plant; large flowers in late spring

R. impeditum—small leaves; purple blue flowers in early April

R. macroleucum—dense blue green tiny foliage; white flowers in spring

R. micranthum—evergreen, spreading foliage; large pink flowers in May

R. myrtifolium—dark leaves that turn purple bronze in fall; pink flowers in May

R. obtusum var. *japonicum*—lavender pink flowers in late April and May; hardy plant

R. racemosum—leathery leaves; cherry clusters of flowers in April and May; slow growing

Salix purpurea var. *nana*—finely toothed leaves; lovely shape

S. uva-ursi—tiny oval leaves with large purple catkins in early spring before leaves appear; small plant

Spiraea bullata—rose-colored flowers in midsummer; twelve to fifteen inches high

S. compacta (arguta)—slightly taller than *Spiraea bullata* with white blooms

Ground Covers:

For bottle gardens and dish gardens, in rock gardens, and in landscapes with dwarf plants, ground cover is the magic green wand that completes a scene. It is the miniaturist's best natural material for pulling a picture together.

A ground-cover plant may be low and branching, a thick mass of leaves, or a colorful cover of tiny flowers. It may be a lush green carpet or a rampant invasive grower. There are hundreds of them, and, although they are mainly considered as replacements for lawns, we shall examine them for use in dish gardens and as companion plantings for dwarf shrubs and trees.

Little pockets of chamomile (*Anthemis nobilis*) or baby's tears (*Helxine soleirolii*) and Corsican mint (*Mentha requienii*) are lovely accents in dish gardens and terrariums. Shrubs such as *Juniperus*

Dwarf trees and shrubs are fine accents in the front landscape plan of this house.
Photo by California Association of Nurserymen.

conferta and *J. horizontalis* are perfect for the garden with dwarf trees.

Ground-cover plants are inexpensive and easy to care for, and they come in a variety of textures and forms. Here are only a few of the many available.

Alyssum wulfenianum
Anthemis nobilis (chamomile)
Arabis
Arctostaphylos uva-ursi (bearberry)
Arenaria verna var. *caespitosa* (Irish moss)
Asperula odorata (sweet woodruff)
Gaylussacia brachycera (box huckleberry)
Genista sagittalis
Helxine soleirolii (baby's tears)
Herniaria glabra
Juniperus conferta
J. horizontalis
Lavandula officinalis (lavender)
Mentha requieni (Corsican mint)

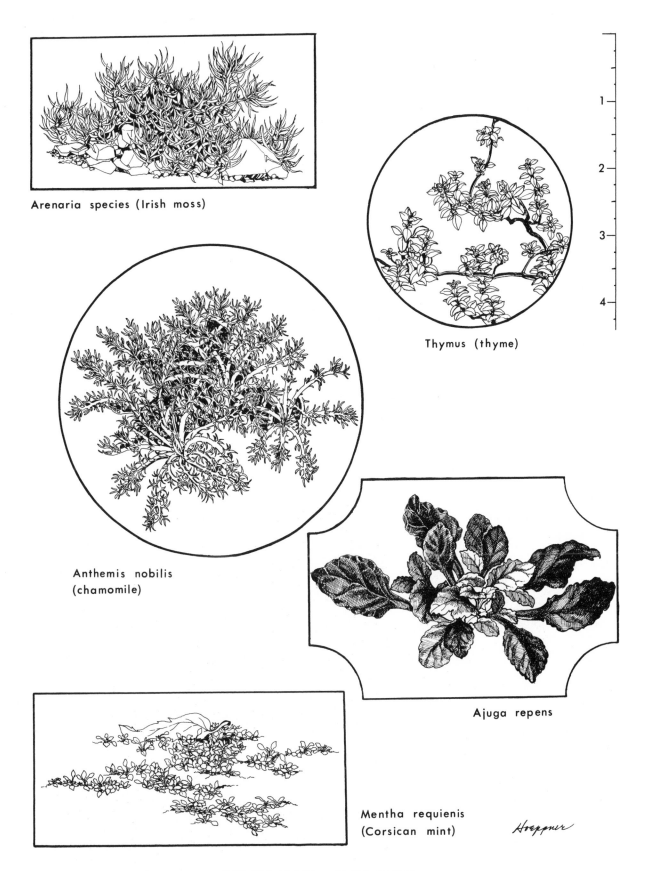

Arenaria species (Irish moss)

Thymus (thyme)

Anthemis nobilis
(chamomile)

Ajuga repens

Mentha requienis
(Corsican mint)

Hoeppner

GROUND COVERS

Nepeta hederacea (ground ivy)
Thymus herba-barona
Vaccinium crassifolium
Veronica allinoii
V. filiformis
V. repens

Ice Plants:

Ice plants were formerly sold as mesembryanthemum; they have now been reclassified.

Cephalophyllum "Red Spike" (*Cylindrophyllum speciosum*)—three to five inches high; fine red flowers
Delosperma "Alba" (white ice plant)—dark green leaves with white flowers
Drosanthemum floribundum—tiny gem with pink or purple bloom
Malephora luteula (*Hymenocyclus*)—fine textured with yellow blooms

This small garden area uses dwarf trees and shrubs to fill the plan. Photo by author.

9. Miniature Plants for Wall Gardens and Sink Gardens ✐

Garden walls are charming assets in the landscape. Many times they are purely decorative; often they are necessary as retaining walls. These barriers need not be barren, for there are dozens of fine miniature plants to make them blaze with color and texture.

Planted horizontally with roots in pockets between the rocks or stones, miniatures offer unique accent for garden walls.

Although dry walls—those put together without cement—are best for miniature plants, even mortared walls can be home for them. Chink out some of the concrete (not all of it) to provide spaces for the plants; in a few months roots will take hold and plants will thrive.

Sink gardening is another ideal way to grow miniatures. Outdoors in old sink or horse troughs placed on pedestals, these are fascinating and always attractive accents in the garden. Since it is difficult to find old sinks or suitable containers, rocks with natural pockets can be used or you can make your own stone containers.

WALL GARDENS

A masonry wall imparts an old world charm to the garden and, studded with small rockery plants, it is decorative, too. Once established, this garden is ridiculously simple to maintain; it will take care of itself for years. However, it takes time to get it started, because plants must be carefully placed in pockets between the rocks without harming their root systems. Watering at first must be thorough and constant. (It is best to sprinkle the wall several times a day to get plants started.)

Be sure to select plants that will thrive in rocklike conditions.

Wall gardens become living tapestries with miniature sempervivums; in a short time they anchor themselves to the stone. Photo by Wayside Gardens.

Many small cacti and succulents are ideal, as are arabis (rockcress) and aquilegia (columbine). Design is not important in the wall garden; put plants in place and allow them to grow. Trim and prune as necessary to establish an eye-pleasing composition.

CONSTRUCTING A WALL GARDEN

If you are good at jigsaw puzzles, you can try to build a stone or rock wall, because the secret is fitting the irregular shapes and sizes into a pleasing pattern. The stones must be properly fitted together, since their weight and balance alone hold the wall together. For most low walls (two feet or less) a foundation layer is not needed. Start at ground level with a firm wide base, and set the largest and flattest stones in place on the bottom first. Granite or basalt rocks are preferred to sandstone, limestone, or shale, which can crumble in excess moisture and low temperatures.

90

You will need a hammer for chipping stones, a sledgehammer for breaking stones, a spade and a shovel for digging foundations, a trowel (if you are using mortar), a level to check the work as it progresses, and some mason's twine to mark the boundaries.

You can build a wall without or with mortar. The dry wall will not be as durable as the mortar wall, but if it lists a bit it can easily be repaired. It is also a good idea to fill in the area behind the wall with a mound of soil. This makes building the wall easy, for it has something to lean against and provides soil for plant roots reaching from the wall.

Each layer of stone should be absolutely solid before you go on to the next layer. To steady very large stones, use smaller ones under them. As the wall is fitted together, you will notice natural nooks and crannies; these are the places for the plants.

A free-standing stone wall (without soil behind it) will require mortar between the stones and a foundation. A sixteen-inch foundation will support a three-foot wall in climates with 0°F. temperature. You can build this wall, but it is usually best to have it done by a professional mason.

The perennial plants mentioned in Chapter 7 are appropriate for wall gardens and additional choices follow.

Arabis alpina (rockcress)
Arctostaphylos uva-ursi (bearberry)
Arenaria verna (tufted sandwort)
Asperula odorata (sweet woodruff)
Erica carnea (heath)
Euonymus fortunei var. *minimus* (dwarf wintercreeper)
Juniperus horizontalis (creeping juniper)
Sedum album (stonecrop)
S. dasyphyllum (stonecrop)
S. sieboldii (stonecrop)
Sempervivum arachnoideum (spider houseleek)
Thymus serpyllum (creeping thyme)

SINK GARDENS

Sink gardening is growing small plants outdoors in old sinks or horse troughs set on pedestals. These gardens are inviting decora-

Alyssum and Iberis *create a handsome wall in this landscape arrangement.* Photo by Molly Adams.

tions and a boon to the gardener who cannot or doesn't want to squat to tend a ground garden. Sink gardening requires patient handwork, for like terrariums and dish gardens, these miniature landscapes are always on display; even the slightest mistake is more evident in the diminutive scene than in the garden of standard plants.

Unfortunately, the availability of a suitable container deters many people from enjoying this fine hobby. Old sinks and horse troughs are generally impossible to find, but concrete birdbaths and stone-container dishes are available. If four to six inches deep, they certainly can be used. (Or make your own concrete containers.) Other container possibilities are fireplace flue tiles or old food-preserving crocks.

Any container must be strong enough to hold the soil and plants, be weather resistant, have drainage holes, and have some charm. I prefer the square containers (which give more planting space) over the rectangular ones, but either shape is acceptable. A sink garden should be placed on top of a wall or on a pedestal, and should be two or three feet off the ground so that it is easy to tend the plants. You can also use concrete or cement blocks to elevate the garden.

PREPARING THE SINK GARDEN

Cover the bottom of the container with a one-half-inch layer of tiny stones and add peat moss to cover them. Now put in soil to about one-third the depth of the container. Press the soil in place to eliminate air pockets and shape the landscape with hills and valleys. Move the potted plants around in the garden until you have the right arrangement. Take the plants from the pots and set them permanently in place. Add small stones, paths, a thin carpet of moss perhaps, and some ground cover to cascade over the container edges. It is wise to follow a basic theme when planting the garden—these are similar to the woodland, desert, or bog landscape used for dish gardens.

PLANTS FOR THE SINK GARDEN

Nature has given us a treasure house of miniature plants for sink gardens—annuals, biennials, perennials, bulbs, shrubs, and trees (see Chapters 7 and 8). Suppliers of alpine and rockery plants offer an infinite variety, and small shrubs and trees can be obtained from bonsai nurseries. Since the beauty of the small sink garden is in its textures and shapes, select picturesque plants that fit the scheme of the landscape.

Small succulents are tucked in wall pockets of this garden; in a few months they will take hold and provide bright color and handsome texture. Photo by Hort Pix.

A concrete block wall uses echeverias as a handsome decoration; ground cover in a handsome tracery grows between the blocks.
Photo by Hort Pix.

Most of the plants are easy to grow if initial good planting procedures have been followed. Once established, these plants will last many years, although pruning and shaping have to be done regularly.

Care

Remember that a planted sink garden is heavy. If possible, put the container where you want it and prepare it there. Put the garden in a place protected from direct sunlight and hot dry winds. (An ideal spot is under a high tree; the branches screen out harmful sunlight, and yet ample light reaches the plants.) If you are growing woodland plants that need shade, a more protected and more moist location is advisable.

The safest general rule for watering the sink garden is the same as for watering house plants: never let the soil get bone dry and never give it so much water that it becomes soggy. The watering frequency will depend on the size and type of container, the soil, the weather, and, of course, the plants themselves.

Plants in fresh soil do not need feeding for over a year and, even then, apply fertilizer moderately. Feed established gardens only twice a year—in early spring and in summer. Remember the joy of the garden is in its miniature proportions, so do not try to force plants into rampant growth.

In severe winter areas, gardens will have to be moved indoors. I find the best site is an unheated garage where there is some light and good air circulation. Or if you prefer, you can protect the plants with salt hay or moss. In any case, the soil should not freeze solidly and crack the container. In mild climates gardens can be outdoors year-round without special weather protection.

A small stone is home for these fine succulents; the miniatures can stay in this "container" for several years.
Photo by Joyce R. Wilson.

10. Miniature Garden Bulbs ✍

There is a special joy in growing such miniature bulbs as snowflakes and grape hyacinths, perhaps because they are not as frequently seen as their larger cousins. Yet this small-plant fairyland offers some enchanting overlooked species that are almost carefree, and even people with only a tiny garden can enjoy them. There is a wealth of charm in these miniatures, and no better way to have spring at your doorstep. Bulbs are pretty indoors and radiant outdoors, where they can be naturalized in nooks and crannies and soon increase to create splashes of color. Choose a moist, partially shady place for them under a large tree or near a rock grouping, or create your own little garden with stepping stones, ground covers, and a spiraling of gravel chips or fir bark. Bulbs are also effective tucked into rock gardens, where bright spots of color are always welcome, and indoors potted bulbs make cheerful and bright table decorations.

The tulip and daffodil miniatures rival their bigger relatives in beauty. Other miniatures are only available in small versions; these include blue crocus and snowdrops that bear nodding white flowers. With bulbs all the work is done for you; they merely have to be placed in the ground at the right time to yield a bounty of flowers.

Some bulbs are hardy and will survive winter, but others must be lifted and stored prior to freezing weather. The summer-flowering bulbs are tender and should be planted in late spring; hardy bulbs such as the popular colchicums and crocus should be planted in late fall, when the plants are dormant.

Dig a deep pocket of six to eight inches and place bulbs in a rich soil. Be sure the site has good drainage, because a soggy soil will

Miniature and dwarf tulips (Tulipa dasystemon) *provide brilliant accent in the garden; plant them in groups for a fine show.* Photo by Wayside Gardens.

quickly rot the bulbs. Generally, planting depth for bulbs is twice the diameter of the bulb. While the bulbs are dormant, too much moisture is not needed; when growth starts or is ripening, the bulbs need moisture. Feeding is not necessary; bulbs have their own stored nutrients, so fertilizing is a waste of time and money.

For a real splash of color, group many bulbs in one area. Sparse planting gives a spotty effect, and it will take several years to create the catalog picture we all strive for. Since bulbs are generally inexpensive, you can be extravagant.

Bulbs for Landscaping:

Chionodoxa (glory-of-the-snow)—from the lily family; pretty open-faced flowers in April; grassy leaves that die after blooms fade (thrives in most soils, but needs bright light)

C. sardensis—deep blue flowers, many to a stem

C. tmoli (*tmolusii*)—late-blooming species with pale blue flowers

Colchicum (meadow saffron)—often called crocus, but members of the lily family; purple or white flowers in late fall (needs a loamy soil and some sunlight)

C. *autumnale* var. *minor*—soft pink flowers; good grower
C. *autumnale* var. *minor album*—pure white; six inches high
C. "Water Lily"—outstanding double pink; six inches high

Crocus—grassy-leaved plants from the iris family; some for spring
bloom and some for fall; many kinds, all desirable (check with
your local nursery)
C. *speciosus* var. *globosus*—bright blue flowers in October
C. *zonatus (kotschyanus)*—large lavender flowers; floriferous

Cyclamen—cousin of florist cyclamens; very fine plants that should
be grown more; generally evergreen through winter, then drop
their leaves before flowers open; bloom time is variable (needs
perfect drainage and shallow planting)
C. *atkinsii*—crimson flowers in January; one of the best, always
popular
C. *neapolitanum*—silver-zoned foliage and rosy pink flowers; popular and highly recommended

Hyacinthus (hyacinth)—small replicas of larger hyacinths; very
charming in concentrated masses (needs rich soil and good drainage)

Tulipa sylvestris.
Photo by Wayside Gardens.

Left: *Chionodoxa is another fine small bulb for gardens.* Photo by Wayside Gardens.

Right: *Hyacinths are lovely indoor bulbs and add seasonal color to the home.* Photo by Wayside Gardens.

H. amethystinus—flat leaves and nodding blue flowers on short spikes

H. azureus (ciliatus)—three-inch spikes; blue green leaves with fine blue flowers

Leucojum (snowflake)—long leaves and nodding bell flowers; easy to grow in almost any soil; overlooked, worthwhile plants

L. aestivum var. *gravetype*—improved form with drooping white flowers tinged with green; can grow to eighteen inches

Muscari (grape hyacinth)—blooms from March through May; fine, small plants with clusters of grapelike blooms; easy to grow in a well-drained rich soil

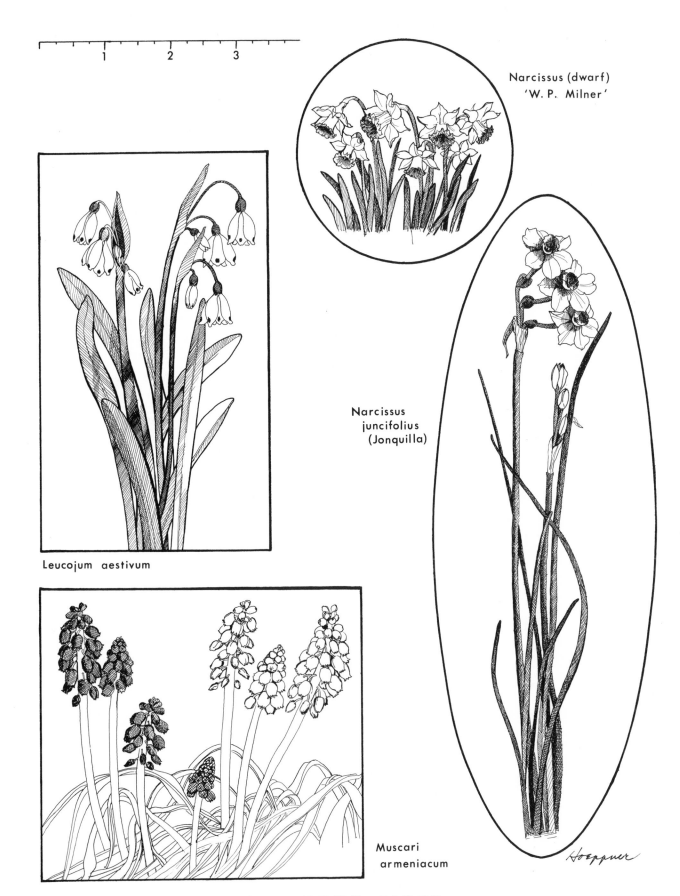

Narcissus (dwarf)
'W. P. Milner'

Narcissus
juncifolius
(Jonquilla)

Leucojum aestivum

Muscari
armeniacum

Hoeppner

MINIATURE BULBS

M. armeniacum—violet blue blooms; free flowering

M. botryoides var. *album*—fine fragrant white flowers in April

M. comosum var. *plumosum*—lavender beauties

M. paradoxum—deep blue flowers; outstanding

Narcissus (daffodil)—many fine miniatures (To my eye, many are superior to their larger relatives, and I wouldn't be without them. There are an infinite number of small daffodils, one prettier than the other, and many have been overlooked. Take the time to investigate this group of plants.)

N. bulbocodium (hoopskirt daffodil)—lovely yellow flowers; many varieties

N. cyclamineus—about four inches high; fine yellow blooms

N. juncifolius (jonquilla)—only three inches tall; scented yellow flowers

N. minimus—smallest trumpet daffodil; rich yellow flowers in February

N. triandrus var. *alba* (angel's tears)—exquisite tiny species with creamy white flowers

Scilla (squill)—charming plants for spring bloom; blue, white, or rose blooms; easy to grow in moist, shady places

S. bifolia var. *rosea*—star-shaped, pale pink blooms

S. sibirica—popular species with fine blue blooms

S. tubergeniana—lovely blue flowers in February or March

Tulipa (tulip)—small plants with bright showy flowers; many varieties—only a few listed (If you have missed these diminutive darlings of the tulip world, you are in for a pleasant surprise.)

T. aucheriana—dainty, scented, orange pink flowers

T. batalinii—primrose yellow flowers in April

T. biflora—white star-shaped flowers with yellow base

T. kaufmanniana—large yellow and red flowers; very showy

T. tarda (dasystemon)—fine yellow for May bloom

MINIATURE BULBS INDOORS

Indoors, where a bright show of flowers is needed, you can have golden daffodils three inches tall or bright crocuses in the middle of winter. Put six or eight bulbs to a five-inch pot in October or early November (most suppliers list them as specially treated for forcing indoors). Use a potting soil of two parts loam, two parts sand, and one part leaf mold. The length of rooting and potting time depends on the variety.

Shallow clay pots are ideal for miniature bulbs, since they have shallow root systems. Put stones or broken pot pieces over the drainage hole and then add adequate soil mix. Set bulbs in place with just the tips barely showing; then thoroughly moisten the soil. Store the pots in a cool dark place at 40° to 50°F., so that premature growth will not be encouraged. A cellar or unheated but not freezing garage is an ideal storage place. Keep soil evenly moist.

You can also force bulbs outdoors for indoor bloom. Sink pots in a trench and cover with salt hay or put containers in a cold frame. When the pots are filled with roots (check the drainage holes to determine this), move the bulbs to a cool shady place in the house for a few days. Then move them to a bright window; keep cool (about 60°F.).

Scilla sibirica *make a lovely planting in this garden.* Photo by Wayside Gardens.

Tulipa kolpakowskiana. Photo by Wayside Gardens.

Bulbs for Forcing Indoors:

Colchicum (meadow saffron)
Crocus
Cyclamen neapolitanum
Hyacinthus (hyacinth)
Muscari (grape hyacinth)
Narcissus (daffodil)
Tulipa

Other small bulbs not often seen, for forcing, are brodiaea, calochortus, and chionodoxa.

104

11. Miniature Water Gardens ✑

Even a small pot of water adds another dimension of beauty to a garden. A water accent used as a mirror to reflect trees and sky is charming; so is a tiny pool with miniature water lilies or other small exotic aquatic plants. The variety of plants for pools is far more plentiful today than even a few years ago.

The little water garden will never duplicate the formal pools of Victorian times, so do not be misled. We are talking here about pools to twenty inches in diameter—rarely impressive, but certainly beautiful. A bowl or dish with water and plants, placed strategically at the end of a bench or in the landscape where paths meet, is an exciting accent in the garden and is so easy to accomplish.

Bowls, Dishes, Tubs, and Buckets

Prefabricated bowls can be purchased at nurseries and come in many materials—stone, metal, plastic, and concrete. Buckets and tubs, also at suppliers, can be used for small pools; they are moderately priced and will last for years. Discarded laundry tubs and other salvaged items are also suitable containers, or, if you prefer, make your own cast-concrete small pools. With small pools there is no need to drain water or install plumbing facilities; change the water by hosing the pool in early spring.

Dishes and bowls are shallow, so you will not be able to grow most water lilies which need a depth of about twenty inches of water, but there are other aquatic plants you can try (listed at the end of chapter). Bucket and tub gardens are popular; these containers, made of tough fiberglass, will accommodate a few lilies for several years.

The maximum size is twenty-four inches at the top tapering to twenty inches at the bottom and twenty inches deep. Fill it with eight to ten inches of soil with a water depth over the crowns of the plants of eight to ten inches.

Careful pool placement is essential, if you want them to be effective. Search for nooks and unused corners where there is a natural landscape, for with proper foliage backgrounds the little pools can become handsome surprise accents. But remember that they must appear as if they belong to the scene rather than as afterthoughts. To make them look natural, sink containers to the rim in the ground and frame them with finely crushed gravel or lush low ground-cover plants.

Dishes and bowls can also be used above ground; since all edges will be exposed, select containers with attractive ornamental rims. Keep these pools simple rather than embellished with background plantings. A few pot plants adjacent to the pool or perhaps a few rocks are all that is needed.

Generally, place dishes near the patio or terrace or by a walkway or path, rather than out in the garden as a central feature. These are charming accents that depend on intimacy and surprise; they are not landscape features.

MINIATURE WATER LILIES AND OTHER AQUATICS

It is hard to resist the beauty of water lilies because they are exotic flowers that brighten any summer scene. Divided into two classes— the hardy type and the tropicals—there are thousands of wonderful varieties, but the majority are large plants and need ample pool space. However, there are several for small pools and, even if you only want them for a season, lilies are worthwhile.

The hardy type is easy to grow; the tropicals, which produce large blooms, are somewhat more demanding. In most climates they are treated as annuals, bought new each spring and discarded in the fall. Hardy lilies die back in winter and in deep water will safely carry over for next spring.

An attractive city garden uses a small water pool as an accent; floating plants decorate the water surface. Photo by Joyce R. Wilson.

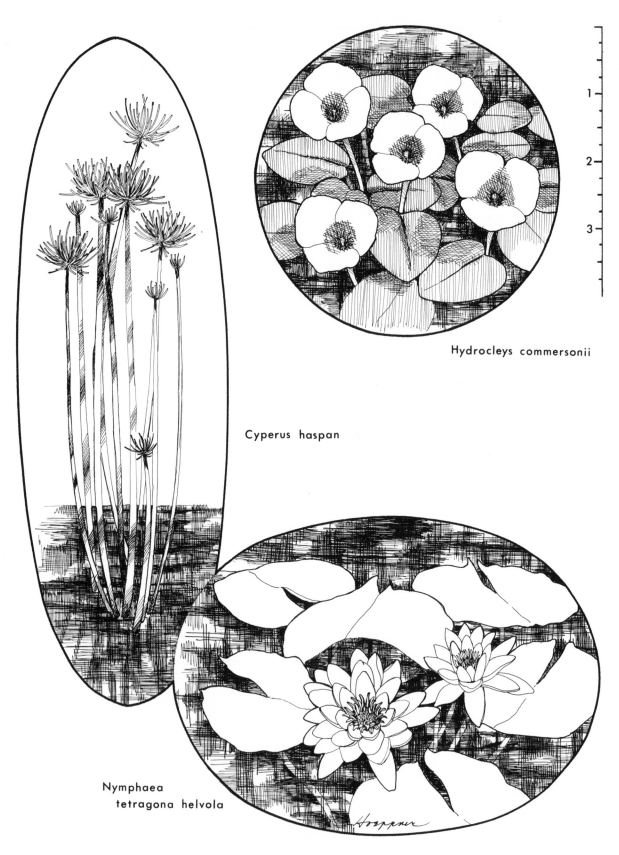

Hydrocleys commersonii

Cyperus haspan

Nymphaea
tetragona helvola

DWARF WATER PLANTS

Miniature water lilies grow without care in a bucket garden. Photo by author.

The water depth for lilies should be at least twenty-four inches, although this varies. They require about twelve inches of soil and a foot of water above them. In most cases tubs or buckets will accommodate only one or two lilies; even the smaller varieties need ample space for peak growth. Lilies are heavy feeders and need a balanced fertilizer in the soil when they are planted and again in July. Wrap fertilizer in small cloth bags and insert two or three into the soil around the lily.

Lilies are shipped in early spring and should be started immediately. Prepare a rich humusy soil (do not add peat or sphagnum.) Set the tubers in place horizontally, about one inch below the soil. Use tepid water for the plants; cold water will harm them. (Many growers suggest water that has been standing a few days.) As water evaporates in tubs or buckets, replace it so that there is always a good water depth. Do not try the small lilies in anything less than a ten-inch container; they just will not respond.

Water Lilies for Tub Gardens

Nymphaea:
   "Aurora"
   "Gloriosa"
   "Hermine"
   "Indiana"
   "Joanne Pring"
   "Mary Patricia"
   "Paul Hariot"
   "Pink Laydekeri"
   Pygmaea helvola (Nymphaea tetragona helvola)
   "Red Laydekeri"
   "White Laydekeri"

Tropical Lily:
   "Blue Pygmae"
   "Frances B. Griffith"
   "Leopardess"
   "Royal Purple"
   "Zanzibar Blue"

Other Aquatics:

Azolla
Elodea
Hydrocleys commersonii (Limnocharis humboldtii; water poppy)
Nymphoides indicum (water snowflake)
N. peltatum (floating heart)

WHERE TO BUY MINIATURE PLANTS

Alberts & Merkel Bros., Inc.
P.O. Box 537
Boynton Beach, Fla. 33435

Orchids, bromeliads, and other tropical plants; catalog $.50

Arthur Eames Allgrove
North Wilmington, Mass. 01887

Terrariums, bottle gardens, and plants; catalog $.25

Antonelli Bros.
2545 Capitola Rd.
Santa Cruz, Calif. 95010

Gesneriads and begonias

Barrington Greenhouses
860 Clements Bridge Road
Barrington, N.J. 08016

House plants

Buell's Greenhouses
Eastford, Conn. 06242

Gesneriads

Burgess Seed & Plant Co., Inc.
67 E. Battle Creek St.
Galesburg, Mich. 49053

Many kinds of miniature plants

W. Atlee Burpee Co.
Riverside, Calif. 92502

Seeds and bulbs

Conrad-Pyle
West Grove, Pa. 19390

Miniature roses

P. De Jager & Sons, Inc.
188 Ashbury St.
S. Hamilton, Mass. 01982

Outstanding selection of bulbs

Fennell Orchid Co.
26715 S.W. 157 Avenue
Homestead, Fla. 33030

Wide selection of orchids; catalog $.50

Fischer Greenhouses
Linwood, N.J. 08221

African violets and other ges-neriads

Goodwill Garden
Route 1
Scarborough, Maine 04074

Alpines

Ben Haines
1902 Lane
Topeka, Kans. 60664

Cacti and succulents; list $1.00

Hauserman's Orchids
Box 363
Elmhurst, Ill. 60218

Wide selection of species orchids

Alexander Irving Heimlich
71 Burlington St.
Woburn, Mass. 01801

Bulbs

Margaret Ilgenfritz
P.O. Box 665
Monroe, Mich. 48161

Large selection of species orchids; catalog $1.00

Kartuz Greenhouses
92 Chestnut St.
Wilmington, Mass. 01887

Miniature plants, especially bromeliads

Logee's Greenhouses
55 North St.
Danielson, Conn. 06239

All kinds of miniature plants; catalog $.50

Lyndon Lyon
14 Mutchler St.
Dolgeville, N.Y. 13329

African violets and columneas

Mayfair Nurseries
U.S. Route 2
Nichols, N.Y. 13812

Dwarf conifers, shrubs, heaths, and heathers

Rod McLellan Co.
1450 El Camino Real
S. San Francisco, Calif. 94080

Orchids

Merry Gardens Camden, Maine 04843	*Complete selection of miniature plants; catalog $1.00*
Oliver Nurseries 1159 Bronson Rd. Fairfield, Conn. 06430	*Evergreens for rock gardens*
Paradise Gardens 14 May St. Whitman, Mass. 02382	*Aquatic plants*
George W. Park Seed Co., Inc. P.O. Box 31 Greenwood, S.C. 29646	*All kinds of miniature plants and seeds*
H. Presner P.O. Box 10 Coral Gables, Fla. 33134	*Bonsai dwarf trees*
Mt. Rainier Alpine Gardens 2007 S. 126 St. Seattle, Wash. 98168	*Dwarf conifers, rhododendrons, and alpines*
Siskiyou Rare Plant Nursery 522 Franquette St. Medford, Oreg. 97501	*Alpines and rock plants; catalog $.50*
Sky-Cleft Gardens Camp St. Ext. Barre, Vt. 05641	*Rock plants*
Slocum Water Gardens 1101 Cypress Garden Rd. Winter Haven, Fla. 33880	*Aquatic plants*
Three Springs Fisheries Lilypons, Md. 21717	*Aquatic plants*
Tinari Greenhouses 2325 Valley Rd. Bethayres, Pa. 19006	*African violets and other plants*

Tropical Paradise Greenhouses
8825 W. 79 St.
Overland Park, Kans. 66200

Wide selection of miniature plants

Van Ness Water Gardens
2460 N. Euclid Ave.
Upland, Calif. 91786

Aquatic plants

Wilson Bros.
Roachdale, Ind. 46172

Geraniums

WHERE TO BUY GLASS CONTAINERS

Arthur E. Allgrove
279 Woburn St.
N. Wilmington, Mass. 01887

Cases, supplies, and figurines

Crystal Glass Tube & Cylinder Co.
7310 S. Chicago Ave.
Chicago, Ill. 60619

Domes and cylinders

Owens-Illinois Glass Co.
Toledo, Ohio 43601

Glass containers of all kinds to the trade only; products available at florist shops

George W. Park Co.
Greenwood, S.C. 29467

Terrariums

A. L. Randall Co.
1325 Randolph St.

Glass containers of all kinds to the trade only; products available at florist shops

West Virginia Glass Specialty Co.
Weston, W.Va. 26452

Glass containers of all kinds to the trade only; products available at florist shops